MY FATH

The cross and the Father's love

Mark Stibbe

For my mum, Joy Stibbe
Eternally grateful to you for adopting me

First published in Great Britain in 2014

Society for Promoting Christian Knowledge
36 Causton Street
London SW1P 4ST
www.spckpublishing.co.uk

British Library Cataloguing-in-Publication Data
A catalogue record for this book is available from the British Library

ISBN 978–0–281–07176–0
eBook ISBN 978–0–281–07177–7

Typeset by Graphicraft Limited, Hong Kong
First printed in Great Britain by Ashford Colour Press
Subsequently digitally printed in Great Britain

eBook by Graphicraft Limited, Hong Kong

Produced on paper from sustainable forests

Contents

Acknowledgements

I have a few brief but heartfelt expressions of thanks to put on record.

First, I am deeply thankful to SPCK, especially Alison Barr, for believing in me enough to invite me to write this volume, and for all the help given in its preparation for publication.

Second, I am extremely grateful to those whom I invited to read the first draft and who offered invaluable insights, especially Hugh and Ginny Cryer and my old friend Professor Andrew Lincoln.

Third, I want to thank those who have worked on the text, especially my copy editor Mollie Barker, who did a fantastic job.

Finally, to the loyal and enthusiastic friends who have been cheering me on as I've tried to put these thoughts on the cross into words: I am forever in your debt.

'I thank my God every time I remember you. In all my prayers for all of you, I always pray with joy because of your partnership in the gospel.'

Philippians 1.3–5

1

The gospel of the heart

My brother says that he only ever saw our father cry on two occasions. The first was when Dad's father died. The second was because of me.

To appreciate just why he shed tears this second time, I need to provide some back story.

My twin sister Claire and I were born to a single-parent mother in Coventry in the autumn of 1960. We were placed in an orphanage in London and then subsequently adopted by Philip and Joy Stibbe. It is Philip Stibbe whom I'm referring to here. He was my adoptive father. And he was a truly remarkable man. Anyone who takes the bold risk to adopt a child is in my view remarkable, heroic even.

But he was also remarkable because of his personality and his experiences. He was without doubt the kindest man I have ever met, and the most patient and dignified. I know this may sound like the kind of romanticized emotion recollected in tranquillity, but it's true. If you had known him, you would have said the same. He had been through immense trials in the Second World War, including three years as a prisoner of war at the hands of the Japanese in Burma, and had met some remarkable people, including C. S. Lewis with whom he had regularly dined when he was a student at Oxford University.

Dad read English Literature at Oxford, enjoying two years there prior to volunteering to serve in the Royal Sussex Regiment, then his final year after he had been liberated in 1945 and repatriated to the UK.

He wouldn't talk much about the terrible suffering he went through. He wrote an eloquent but typically understated book about it all, called *Return via Rangoon*.[1] This highly acclaimed testimony was his sole comment on his years of torment. It was his catharsis. No more needed to be said.

However, when I started to fall in love with English literature in my teens, Dad did on one occasion open up a little more. I was walking the dogs with him in a country park in Norfolk. He was in his early sixties at the time and the onset of Parkinson's disease had not yet been detected.

We began to talk about the English Romantic poets. And he began to share about his time in Rangoon jail, when he must have passed through the gates of hell.

'The only thing that kept me going some days was the poetry I had memorized.'

'How do you mean?' I asked.

'I used to recite poetry when we went out on working parties from the prison.'

'Who was your favourite?'

'Wordsworth,' he answered.

'Where did your fondness for him come from?'

'It was during my time before going to Oxford. I was supposed to be reading Classics. Everything was geared up for that anyway. But I went to the Lake District and fell in love with Wordsworth and decided to read English Literature instead. I'm glad I did.'

And then he began to recite some lines as our boots squelched through the early January mud. On and on he went until he reached the conclusion:

> Nor wilt thou then forget
> That after many wanderings, many years
> Of absence, these steep woods and lofty cliffs,
> And this green pastoral landscape, were to me
> More dear, both for themselves and thy dear sake.[2]

As Dad finished, he remained quiet for several minutes, as did I. He was not a man given to displays of emotion, but I could tell that the words had moved him deeply.

Later I received some comments from an MP who wrote to me about his time at Bradfield College, where Dad had taught English for 27 years.

'I'll never forget it,' the MP wrote. 'Your father had been reading some Milton to us in an English lesson. He was sitting in his black gown at the front of the class. When he came to the end he became so affected by what he had read that he opened up his desk lid and took cover behind it for a few moments as he took out a handkerchief and recovered his poise.'

Making an exhibition of myself

The second time my brother saw my father cry was at the end of a telephone call in 1979.

I had fallen in love with English literature, and Dad had been watching my growing interest with keen and increasingly misty eyes. By the time I was 16 I had published my first book – a collection of poems[3] – and by 17 I had set my heart on reading English at Cambridge University. I had taken my exams and been to my interviews, and now we were all waiting.

Then one night in 1979 the phone in the study started to ring. It was one of those black, Steepletone dial phones with a classic ringtone.

Mum picked up the receiver. 'It's for you,' she whispered to me, barely able to disguise her excitement. 'It's Trinity College,' she added softly in my ear as she passed by.

As I spoke to the tutor for admissions, my mother quietly shepherded the rest of the family to the study door.

'Thanks for letting me know,' I said to the man on the other end of the phone before placing the handset back in its cradle. I turned around and walked out to the foot of the staircase in the hall.

'I've been awarded an exhibition to read English at Trinity,' I said.

I didn't see what happened next because I was in a daze. But my father evidently couldn't stand. He sat down on the stairs, according to my brother.

3

And it was there that Giles saw my father's tears, for the second and the final time in his life.

Our story, God's story

I have written and spoken on many occasions about how influential my adoptive father was in my eventual discovery of the true nature of God's character.[4] That discovery was caught more than taught.

I had not been a person of faith during my teenage years. In fact, I had baulked at the institutional Christian religion of both the schools I attended between 1968 and 1979. I don't mean to be disrespectful, but most of the chaplains didn't exactly light up my soul with enthusiasm for Christianity. The God of their formal and very dry chapel services was the God of the far away – an absent Father who didn't seem to make any visits other than the one his Son had made at the nativity 2,000 years before. Other than that, his imminence was not expected and his transcendence was protected. His affections, if he had any, were hidden in scented wisps of mystery.

Then, to my amazement and the even greater amazement of my rebellious peers, I stumbled one evening upon the person of Jesus Christ, and found that he was and is alive and well. More than that, I learned that Christianity was always meant to be relational more than religious and that God was intentional about friendship with us – so intentional in fact that Jesus Christ had gone to hell and back to bring us into the Father's affectionate embrace.

After years of experiencing God's remoteness, that was both subversive and overwhelming.

But even when I had encountered Jesus, I didn't really understand what he had tried to teach and indeed to show us about the Father. I suppose I subconsciously believed the lie that God was like my earthly father – not my adoptive father, that is, but my biological father. At that time I knew nothing about him.

I didn't know what his name was or what he had done for a job. He was a mystery to me – someone who had disappeared from the scene before my teenage mother gave birth to my twin sister and me. Living in the legacy of that prenatal narrative, I had done what so many do and projected the unknown face of my earthly father onto the equally unknown face of my heavenly Father. My picture of God the Father was therefore impaired. I had effectively constructed him in my biological father's image.

It took a long time for that to be displaced by a more truthful God-image, and it was not formal religion that did this but personal revelation. The truth is that I came to see in quite a dramatic way that God is an immensely kind, long-suffering, loving and perfect Father. He is much more like my adoptive father than my biological father, although even saying that may be committing the error of transference. Our heavenly Father is, after all, so much holier and more affectionate than even our best earthly dads are. He is perfect – simple as that. Even Philip Stibbe wasn't perfect, and he would have been the first to admit it.

In the end it was an encounter with the Holy Spirit that took this picture of God as Father from my head to my heart. Through the Spirit of adoption, my heart was inflamed with a stunning and entirely new revelation: *Thanks to what Jesus has done at Calvary, we can come to see that God is the Father who has adopted us as his royal sons and daughters, and with Spirit-ignited hearts we can know him relationally and speak to him personally.*

Looking at it now, I am sure that the priceless gift of my adoptive father was the single most important factor – outside God himself, of course – in my coming to this life-transforming understanding. Dad never said anything to me about this kind of heavenly Father. But he certainly modelled it. And without his influence, so clearly orchestrated by the providential wisdom of God, I doubt whether I would ever have been able to have understood such things so profoundly or so permanently.

Rediscovering the Trinity

Looking back over the course of my life, I can now see that encountering Jesus and experiencing the Holy Spirit were critical moments in my discovery of the divine Father.

Encountering Jesus was critical because it is hard to even conceive of knowing God as Father outside Jesus Christ. It is still not really properly appreciated how original the *Abba* revelation is to Jesus (i.e. the revelation of God as dearest Father or Papa, the meaning of the Aramaic word *Abba*). Only in Christianity is Jesus worshipped as the one and only Son of God. Only in the Judaeo-Christian tradition is God revealed to be our loving heavenly Father. Jesus Christ is truly the Way to the Father. When a person meets Jesus, he or she discovers the heart-warming truth that God is our affectionate *Abba*.

This alone, however, is not enough to make such a revelation a reality. The nature of Jesus as Son and the teaching of Jesus about God's Fatherhood are objective truths, and we can come to assent to them intellectually. But something more is needed if we are to move from the realm of the objective to the subjective, from the propositional to the personal, from the cognitive to the affectionate.

That 'something more' is the work of the Holy Spirit.

When individuals come to faith in Christ they do so because the Holy Spirit has brought them to a sense of conviction that Jesus Christ is the only Son of God by nature, the Mediator between earth and heaven, the one who has brought us home into the arms of the Father. This work of the Holy Spirit is what opens our hearts up to the reality that God is a Father who loves us with an everlasting love and that we are forever his sons and daughters by adoption.

This is because the primary ministry and task of the Holy Spirit in the believer's life is not only to show us who Jesus really is – the Son by nature – but also to reveal to our spirits who we really are: chosen sons and daughters. And so we cannot do without the Holy Spirit. If the second person of the Trinity opens up a vision of the Father's heart, it is the third person of the Trinity who leads us into that heart in an embrace that sets in motion the possibility of transformation and liberation at every level of our lives.

To experience this is to experience the Trinity.

Rediscovering spiritual adoption

In the development of my Trinitarian faith, one of the most significant moments was when I began to rediscover a much neglected biblical metaphor, that of spiritual adoption. After more than ten years as a Christian, I had never heard a single sermon or talk on this subject. Converted into a strict, conservative evangelical Christianity, the emphasis was on justification. Never once did I hear my teachers or my peers talking about the glorious Pauline picture of our adoption in Christ. What took precedence was a legal narrative – a narrative in which God is judge, we are lawbreakers, but Christ's death had paid the punishment that satisfied the Father's demand for justice.

Then, one evening, I encountered what John Wesley called 'the loving Spirit of adoption'. Suddenly my eyes were opened. God is not primarily a judge. He's first and foremost an adopting, affectionate Father.

That changed everything.

I went back to the Scriptures and discovered that on five occasions the apostle Paul had used the word *huiothesia*, literally 'the placing of a son', translated in most versions as 'adoption'.[5] Further research uncovered that Paul had been using a picture from the Roman world. He was a Roman citizen so Roman adoptions were familiar to him. When a Roman couple wanted to adopt a son, they did so because they wanted to continue the *paterfamilias*, the family tree on the husband's side. To preserve his legacy, the husband would very likely adopt the son of a slave in his own extended household.

The actual rite of an adoption involved two stages. First, the adopting father would go with the enslaved father to a magistrate.

They would take the potential adoptee, the young boy, with them. A sale would then take place. Three times the adopting father would purchase the enslaved child with gold and silver. After the third sale the transaction would be complete. All this would take place before seven witnesses.

Then the second stage would occur. The magistrate would declare that the boy was now the actual heir of the new adopting father. He would decree that the child was no longer under the *patria potestas* – the fatherly authority – of the enslaved father but under his new father's authority. He would also rule that all the boy's prior debts were now cancelled.

When I discovered this, my heart leaped. What a moving picture Paul had found, under the enlightenment of the Holy Spirit, to explain our salvation in Christ! Before Christ came, we had been slaves. We had been in debt. We had been insecure. We had had no future. But now that Christ has come, we have been bought out of slavery, not through gold and silver but through his own precious blood. Consequently, we are no longer slaves but sons. We are no longer in debt but co-inheritors with Christ. We are adopted. We have a new Father, a new family, a new future.

When I rediscovered this forgotten truth, my whole perspective changed. The court that I had been taught about in the legal version of Christianity was in fact an adoption court! Thanks to Jesus, I had become an adopted son of God.

Models of the atonement

My encounter with the Spirit of adoption changed my theology as radically as my actual adoption had changed my life. From this moment on, I could never read the Bible in the same way. Nor could I understand the cross as I had done.

This is in no way to disparage or dismiss other ways of looking at the cross. I have always believed that there is no single, central metaphor or model of the atonement in the New Testament but rather a kind of *assiette de gourmandises* – a wonderful array of colourful and nourishing options from which the believer can choose as she or he seeks to feed on the great benefits of Calvary.

In my view, there have always been at least five main metaphors of the atonement, and these are sacrificial, commercial, martial, legal and political in character.

First of all, there is the sacrificial metaphor, rooted in the sacrifices of the Jewish Temple, in which Jesus becomes the sacrifice for our sins at Calvary. Christ's sacrifice, unlike those of the Old Covenant, is permanent and universal. It is once and for all. Thanks to what Jesus Christ has done on the cross, we can be forgiven, receive God's mercy, and experience 'at-one-ment' with the Father.

Second, there is the commercial metaphor, rooted in the slave markets of the first century AD, in which Jesus becomes the ransom for many. In this picture Jesus is the one who buys us out of slavery to sin and to the law, and brings us into the freedom of knowing God as his children. The price for this redemption is not gold or silver but Christ's precious blood, by which we are liberated from the devil's hold.

This brings us next to the martial metaphor, rooted in the battlefield, in which Christ becomes our Victor through his death. Living a totally righteous life, Jesus took the full condemnation for our inability to keep the Torah. The enemy has always been the one accusing us, condemning us for not measuring up. When the enemy orchestrated Christ's death, he orchestrated his own defeat. Thanks to Jesus' taking our condemnation, we can now live with the glorious realization that there is no charge or accusation against us. The enemy has been defeated!

Mention of charges brings us to the legal metaphor, rooted in the law court, in which Christ's sacrificial death results in a 'not guilty' sentence. More than that, it results in the declaration that those who are now in Christ are 'in the right'. Thanks to Christ's death, a miraculous exchange has taken place. Christ receives all our unrighteousness in his body on the cross. We receive his righteousness by faith. We therefore enjoy an unmerited pardon – a pardon that ends the hostility between us and God, and brings us heavenly *shalom* or peace.

This reference to peace brings us to the fifth and final metaphor, which is political in nature. In this light, the cross is seen to secure reconciliation not just vertically (with God) but also horizontally (with each other). Through the blood of Christ, the dividing wall of hostility between nations (especially between Jews and Gentiles) has been destroyed. What the politicians couldn't do, Christ did! Through his sacrificial death, Christ brings an end to historical enmities and creates a new humanity in which we all have access to the Father.

These five prevailing metaphors, however much they have been subjected to revisionist interpretations in recent decades, still have life for countless Christians.

But there is another metaphor which I believe has received precious little attention, and that is the metaphor of adoption. In this picture, Christ in his death pays the price required for us to be rescued out of our orphan state – characterized by servitude and striving – and into the new and glorious position as the sons and daughters of our Father in heaven. Through the blood that he sheds at Calvary, our older Brother enters this alienated planet and does for us what we could not do for ourselves – leads us out of the orphanage to the Father's house.

This is a metaphor that is rooted in the home. It was exploited by the apostle Paul with inspirational creativity. Looking at salvation history, he understood by revelation that God is the adopting Father whose Son paid the price for us to be set free from a life of slavery (the performance-based life of the spiritual orphan), so that we could enjoy the glorious freedom of the adopted sons and daughters of God.

This picture of adoptive love, I want to propose, is both an intimate and a vital metaphor. It is intimate because, while all the other five metaphors are relational, the metaphor of adoption is *familial*. In this narrative, we become sons and daughters who know God with that same intimacy with which Jewish children know their *Abba*. We are welcomed into the family of the Trinity as daughters and sons.

And it is vital – both in the sense of 'living' and 'important' – because this is a metaphor that has life in a world like ours, where millions of children are aching for adoption and where on every continent human beings are pining because they have lacked the love of a father. In fact, I would argue that never has there been a more opportune or urgent time for reinstating the adoption metaphor.

The gospel of the cross

All the above discussion is background for this present volume which I have called *My Father's Tears* (with apologies to John Updike[6]).

After over two decades of speaking and writing about the Fatherhood of God, I have come to the conclusion that there are many Christians who live with a deep-seated and agonizing sense of the remoteness of God. In too many eyes, the first person of God is a distant Father, often an absent Father, sometimes even an abandoning Father. This has affected everything people believe, including what they believe about the cross. This stands to reason if you think about it. How you picture God will radically influence how you understand what was going on at Calvary. If you picture God as a conquering king, then you will understand the cross in militaristic terms. If you understand God as a judge, then you will understand the cross in juridical terms. Theology – the God-concept and the God-image in your intellectual operating system – affects everything.

It is here that we come to the main point and purpose of *My Father's Tears*. It is my conviction that we haven't paid anything like enough attention to the theology of God's Fatherhood. His affectionate, affirming, adoptive love is at the very epicentre of his nature. While there are many other names for God (such as Warrior, Judge and King), the title 'Father' is his Christian name.

Only in the Bible is he revealed as a perfect, loving, heavenly Father. As has been pointed out many times before, Islam has 99 names for God, but the one missing is 'Father'. *Abba* is the name on Jesus' lips alone. It should be on the Christian's lips too. Every morning we should be crying, '*Abba*, Father'; every night too.

This God-image and God-concept, once it has been truly embedded in the human soul, transforms our view of everything, including the cross. If the primary truth about God is the truth that he is an extravagantly self-giving adoptive Father – a Father who will do anything to draw orphans home into his eternal embrace – then this has to impact the way we look at what was going on at Calvary. If the lens through which we look is the lens of the Father's love – what I call 'the Love of all loves' – then while we may respect other perspectives of the cross, our view will be *familial*.

More than anything else, such a view will focus on the way the human heart of Jesus endured the agony of abandonment by his Father at Calvary in order to lead us out of the orphanage into the healing warmth of the Father's embrace.

It will focus on the way God the Father suffered the searing pain of bereavement as he saw his Son suffer and die so that we could be led back from the far country into the eternal security of his house.

It will focus finally on the way the Holy Spirit makes these truths real in our hearts, and turns us away from being religious slaves and towards our heart's true home – which is what the Bible calls 'sonship' (which of course includes daughters).

This, in a nutshell, is why I have written *My Father's Tears*. I want to propose that the gospel will be most effectively communicated in this postmodern generation by those who see and describe the story of the cross in terms that honour the biblical picture of God as an adopting Father and us as spiritual orphans, separated from his love, but brought home by our older Brother's sacrifice.

My aim, therefore, is to show you your Father's tears. It is to take you back to the event of the cross and to try in my own finite and faltering words to show you what was going on between the Father and the Son, and the Son and his Father, at the Place of the Skull.

I am going to urge you to give attention to the biblical revelation of God's Fatherhood and the neglected doctrine of adoption as you seek to understand and share the gospel. In the process, I am going to make an attempt at telling the same story – the story of the cross – from an unfamiliar yet liberating angle. I will show you the grieving Father and the abandoned Son, and propose that in this excruciating picture we will find the gospel for our fatherless generation.

This, I believe, is the heart of the gospel.

When we rediscover it, we will find that it is the gospel of the heart.

2

Tears from heaven

What happened in your soul when I started speaking in the last chapter about God as Father?

Did you rage against such talk? Did you rail against the very notion of a God trapped within such paternalistic and masculine language?

Or did it tap into a primal wound? Did you have a sigh in your heart and say to yourself, 'I long to know God in this way, but I don't understand what it means to be fathered like this'?

Or did you sneer at the idea? Did you resist the very notion of God, driven by an inner compulsion to deny that this Father even exists? Did you want to go beyond atheism to anti-theism – to believing against the very idea of the Father?

Or did you sense an inner resonance, a sense of fit, a heart-warming connection? Did your heart sing at the very word 'Father'?

When metaphors die

Having spoken and written on this subject for nearly a quarter of a century, I have come to realize that there are countless people for whom the very idea of God's Fatherhood is deeply problematic. To some it is even a stumbling block, a seemingly intractable obstacle to intimacy with God.

There are many reasons why this might be, but the most common is the one I mentioned in the last chapter. Most of us tend to project the faces of our own flawed fathers onto God. This proclivity towards transference leads to defective images and concepts of God. So, for example:

If you had an angry father, you may conceive of God as volatile, unpredictable, stern and quick to anger.

If you had a father who abandoned you, you may feel that you can't quite trust God not to do the same.

If you had a father who abused you, you may see God as a Father whose touch you'd rather avoid at any cost.

If you had a father who didn't keep his promises to you, you may come to believe that God isn't trustworthy.

If you had a father who was stingy, you may have problems with the idea of God's lavish generosity.

If you had a father who was sick and weak, you may find it difficult to picture a strong, almighty Father.

If you had a father whose death traumatized you, you may struggle to see God as a Father who is truly alive.

If you had a father who lived apart from you, you may feel that God can only be rarely encountered.

If you had a father who was emotionally absent, you may tend to think of God as disengaged and detached.

See how the equation is set up? Hurt by an earthly father, we become suspicious of our heavenly Father.

Our 'father-wounds' therefore gravely debilitate us. They cause us to project our memories of being poorly fathered onto God. We then wander perpetually in a land of spiritual deprivation – a land in which the living metaphor of God's fatherly love is robbed of all traction in our hearts. Instead of drawing near, we shrink back. Instead of trusting, we are suspicious. Instead of living from a centre of love, we live from a centre of fear.

In all these and other ways, we keep ourselves in chains of religious servitude when we could be relishing the majestic freedom of the children of God.

When the metaphor dies, we die too.

Reversing the projection

There is really only one way we can find freedom from this terrifying descent into fatherless Christianity. That is to reverse the projection. In other words, instead of caving in to our wounded human instincts and projecting our experience of fatherhood onto God, we need to adjust our default settings and do the exact opposite: we need to project God's experience of fatherhood onto ours. Only if we reverse the impulse to transfer from the human to the divine will we become free from the idea and the experience of God's remoteness. Only if we cease from our seemingly relentless tendency to create God in our father's image will we be truly free. Sooner or later we have to face our pain and change our perspective.

We therefore have to make a choice.

The first choice is the choice made by the person who is stuck in the mindset of a spiritual orphan. It is the decision to yield to the gravitational pull of the flesh and to bring God's flawless Fatherhood down to the level of our own experience of being imperfectly fathered.

The second choice is the one made by the person who has bowed to the call to be a son or daughter. It is the decision to surrender to the aerodynamic lift of the Spirit and allow even our worst experiences of fatherhood to be raised up to heaven, where fatherhood is perfectly defined and displayed.

This encouragement to reverse the projection is implied by the apostle Paul when he breaks out once again into prayer in his Letter to the Ephesians. J. B. Phillips translates Ephesians 3.14–19 as follows:

> When I think of the greatness of this great plan I fall on my knees before God the Father (from whom all fatherhood, earthly or heavenly, derives its name), and I pray that out of the glorious richness of his resources he will enable you to know the strength of the spirit's inner re-inforcement – that Christ may actually live in your hearts by your faith. And

I pray that you, firmly fixed in love yourselves, may be able to grasp (with all Christians) how wide and deep and long and high is the love of Christ – and to know for yourselves that love so far beyond our comprehension.[1]

Notice how Phillips renders the opening statement: 'I fall on my knees before God the Father (from whom all fatherhood, earthly or heavenly, derives its name)'. This differs from other translations, such as the New International Version (NIV): 'For this reason I kneel before the Father, from whom every family in heaven and on earth derives its name.' Why does Phillips say 'fatherhood' when the NIV here says 'family'?

The answer is simple. The Greek word in the original can mean either. Phillips decided, because of the context, to translate it as 'fatherhood'. Paul is bowing his knees in prayer to his heavenly Father. Therefore 'fatherhood' is preferable to 'family'.

What did Paul therefore mean when he wrote that all fatherhood derives its 'name' from God the Father?

In the Hebraic mindset, the name of a person is inextricably linked to his or her character. When Paul says that all fatherhood derives its name from God's Fatherhood, he is proposing that all fatherhood derives its character from God's. This means that if we want to know what fatherhood is truly about, we need to look at the way God fathers us. If we want to know what the name 'father' properly denotes, then we need to build a picture from Scripture of the Fatherhood of God.

In short, we need to reverse the projection.

Reconstructing our God-image

How then do we go about this?

It needs to be said from the beginning that this is no simple process. Our predilection for quick-fix solutions won't help us here. We cannot trivialize the healing journey by reducing it into a formula, a series of 'how to' steps, or a set of slick sound bites.

17

The truth is that our father-wounds can take time to heal. There may be critical moments of intervention and liberation, but for the most part this is a long process in which the negative experience of being fathered by men needs to be gently displaced by the positive experience of being fathered by God. When the Holy Spirit, who is the Spirit of adoption, is permitted to attend to the intense hurts of our orphaned hearts, we set in motion the possibility of a profound transformation in the way we think. Once our hearts are tenderly held by the enfolding arms of the Spirit, we can then start to re-imagine God in the light of the scriptural celebration of his fatherly love. Put another way, once the heart submits to the healing work of the Spirit, the mind can then start to reorient itself to the reinvigorating image of the open-armed Father who loves us like no earthly father ever could.

I have written extensively on the healing work to which the heart needs to be exposed in books like *I Am Your Father*, so I suggest you venture there.[2] *My Father's Tears*, however, is more of a theological exploration, one whose purpose is to propose a fresh perspective on the cross of Christ. For this to happen we have to accept that our image of God might need reconstructing. In particular, we may need to accept the possibility that God is not distant or detached like some of our earthly fathers. He is not the God of the ancient Greeks who is defined by *apatheia*, absence of suffering. He is in fact the exact reverse of this Hellenistic aberration. He is sympathetic, not apathetic. He doesn't avoid our pain; he feels it.

In short, God is Immanuel. He is not a deity who is above or against us. He is the Father who is among us.

A perfect likeness

Where can we find the most dependable picture of the Father heart of God?

Before I answer that, it might be helpful to say something again about my own story.

I have already made reference to my adopting father, Philip Stibbe. My twin sister and I were adopted by Philip and Joy Stibbe in 1961. They already had their own son, called Giles. But they couldn't have any other children. Wanting to adopt twins, they embarked on a journey which was given impetus and direction by a godly nun called Sister Thérèse. To cut a long story short, she connected them with Claire and me. Some months later, they came into the orphanage and took us into their arms and into their hearts. A few minutes later we were being driven in the back of a car in two Moses baskets to the house where our soon-to-be brother was eagerly waiting.

Over the next five or six years, Claire and I came to realize that we were different from Giles. Giles was the biological child. We were adopted. Giles was fully aware of this as well. On one occasion he was heard in conversation with his best friend who lived next door.

'My mum's having another baby,' she cried.

'Is it real or is it adocted?' Giles asked. Clearly the word 'adopted' was too much at that stage! But the idea was not beyond him. He knew that he was different. He was 'real', to use his own terminology; Claire and I were 'adocted'. Or, as someone once put it, he came out of Mum's tummy; we came out of Mum's heart.

The point I'm making is that Giles was the son by nature while Claire and I were children by adoption. This became more and more evident as we grew up. Giles looked like our father. He sounded like him too. Indeed, today if I want to remember how my father talked and behaved, I need to go no further than his natural son. Giles is truly like his biological father. He possesses an extraordinary similarity to him.

This kind of differentiation needs to be made with regard to the distinction between us and our Brother Jesus. He is the Son by nature. We who are in Christ are sons and daughters by adoption. If we want to know what the Father is like, it is not primarily at each other that we gaze. It is at Jesus. He is the exact representation and likeness of the Father. He is the Son who truly, reliably and completely reveals what God the Father is like. Without Jesus we would be groping around in the dark. With him we see the Father, because whoever sees Jesus sees the Father (John 14.8).

We cannot therefore have a meaningful theology without a robust Christology. Our ability to grasp who God is and speak about him with clarity depends entirely on our ability to grasp who Jesus is and speak about him with integrity. If I want to know what the Father is like, then, I need to look at and indeed listen to the Son. The Son is the Revealer from heaven. He is the one who reminds us what the Father who transcends time is really like. In the same way, my brother Giles is the one who continues to remind me what my adoptive father, who is now beyond space and time, was really like.

The Son affords a clear view of the Father's love. He is a dependable picture of the Father heart of God.

Feasts for the fallen

In everything that Jesus said and did he revealed what his heavenly Father is like. He did nothing unless he first saw his Father doing it. He said nothing unless he heard the Father first saying it. In both his works and words, Jesus provided a pristine window onto the fatherly heart of God.

Let's begin by looking at his words.

There is no finer and more compelling picture of the Father than in Jesus' most famous parable, often called 'The Parable of the Prodigal Son'. Actually, as has been pointed out many times, the story is not really about the rebellious younger son. It is about the outrageously loving father.

The story itself has a context in its original setting. Jesus tells this story during a debate with some religious legalists who are murmuring about the company he's been keeping. In particular, they are muttering and gossiping about the rabble with which he shares his meals. Tax collectors, sinners, prostitutes – the litter layer of Jewish society – are flocking to his open table.

'If he was the Messiah, he wouldn't be having meals with messed-up people like this!' That was the gist of their murmuring.

Jesus doesn't answer their critique with a well-fashioned, doctrinal argument. He tells a story. In fact, he tells three: a trilogy of parables in which there's a lot of partying when the lost are found.

The third of these stories concerns a lost boy – a son who demands his inheritance while his father is still alive and wanders off to squander it all on what we would today call 'an addictive lifestyle'. The father doesn't run after him but waits at home, praying and pining for the day when his much loved and much missed boy will come shuffling home.

Then one day, he sees the silhouette of a man on the horizon of the desert.

Luke records what happens next: 'But while he was still a long way off, his father saw him and was filled with compassion for him; he ran to his son, threw his arms round him and kissed him' (Luke 15.20).

See what Jesus does here. First of all, he cleverly criticizes his critics through his depiction of the father. This dad believes in embrace, not exclusion. His son is covered in the detritus of the pig pen. He is truly unclean and deserves to be excluded. But the father doesn't tell him to wash and to change his clothes before accepting him back. He runs to him and hugs the hell out of him. Indeed, in the original language, Luke tells us that he falls upon his son's neck.

Second, Jesus subtly portrays a father who goes far beyond what any dad in that culture would have been expected to do. In the shock of that, there is a stunning hint about the purpose of the story. The purpose is not to dwell on the son and reinforce the guilt-edged religion of his audience. It is to focus on the father and subvert the very God-image and God-concept that his listeners have been promoting. Their God is a God of exclusion. His is the God of embrace.

What the Son is doing here, then, is revealing his Father. The accepting, non-judgmental, patient, affectionate, merciful and party-throwing father in the parable is a picture of our Father in heaven. It is the furthest remove possible from the legal misrepresentation of God in the minds and on the lips of Jesus' religiously sophisticated listeners.

This is a familial, not a legal, God.

This is the God who holds banquets for broken people, just like Jesus is doing.

This is the Father that the world has been waiting for. Without Jesus we would never have seen him.

The mourning Messiah

Is it possible to imagine the father in the parable holding back his tears when he sees his son and runs like the wind to intercept him?

It is not.

His intestines were torn the moment he realized that the distant figure was his lost son. That is the essence of Luke's phrase, '[he] was filled with compassion for him'. This is a gut-level response, deeper even than the emotions. It is something primal, visceral and parental. There are really no adequate words to translate it. Consequently we have to fill in the blanks as we imagine the eyes of the running father here. The narrative restraint of Jesus, the Master Storyteller, cries out for this.

The father in the story must, then, have been weeping.

And this means that our heavenly Father weeps too.

If we are in any doubt, we should remember the shortest verse of the Bible. John 11.35 may be small in vocabulary but it is big in theology. As Jesus stands outside the tomb of his much-loved friend Lazarus, John records: 'Jesus wept.'

John's word for 'wept' suggests a much deeper emotional response than the one used of the mourners who are wailing in the vicinity of the Bethany tomb. This verb means not just to weep but to sob. In saying this John doesn't resort to 'telling'. In other words, he doesn't tell us what is going on in Jesus' heart. Like the best storytellers he restricts himself to 'showing'. He simply shows us

Jesus sobbing, but in that very act of showing there is a wealth of suggestion. For in John's Gospel, to see Jesus is to see the Father. Everything Jesus says and does is revelatory. It discloses the Father heart of God. And if Jesus sobs at a funeral 2,000 years ago, that means the Father weeps at our funerals too.

It was for this reason that in the two decades I spent serving as a parish priest I would always speak on John 11.35 and the 'weeping Father' at funeral services. So many mourners at chapels and churches, gravesides and gardens, had been influenced by Greek thinking. Their template was one in which God was remote from their pain, far away from their loss, incapable of feeling what they felt. But in hearing of the mourning Messiah at Lazarus' tomb, their template began to change. They heard about a God who weeps – a Father whose tears fall into the midst of their sorrow. In that revelation there truly is some solace. Though it can never offer an answer to 'why', it can offer an answer to 'what'.

No one can claim to know *why* God allows some of the suffering that we see. But we can all know *what* he is doing when we suffer loss. According to John 11.35, the Father is sobbing too. He knows what it is to be inconsolable with grief. Thanks to the Man of Sorrows, he truly is familiar with our deepest pits of pain.

First things first

What all this indicates is the paramount importance of starting with our image of God before we proceed to the event of the cross. If we begin to look at the Calvary event with a faulty picture of the character of God, we may very likely end up with a distorted view of the atonement. For example, those who believe that God is before anything else a judge will see the cross achieving a legal purpose – a purpose in which Jesus suffers some sort of punitive justice in our place. Those who believe that God is first and foremost a king will see the cross achieving a military purpose – a purpose in which Christ triumphs over the devil through his death. How we see God dictates how we see everything, especially the cross.

Our fundamental God-image and God-concept is accordingly of paramount importance. The way we picture God will radically affect the way we picture the atonement.

This is why God's Fatherhood must come first. For me, the primary living metaphor that defines the very core of God's nature is the apostolic depiction of him as a loving, adopting and affectionate Father. That is his divine identity. He is our Father in heaven.

Immediately we say this, however, we must be careful not to dilute or pollute his Fatherhood by importing ideas taken from our own experiences of being fathered.

He is not a Father who vents his rage at us like human fathers who traumatize their sons and daughters through uncontrolled anger and shameful abuse.

He is not a Father who frowns with disapproval at us like fathers on earth who degrade their children by making them feel as if they are forever a disappointment.

He is not a Father who hides behind the clouds like human fathers who sit behind a tabloid or a tablet, disengaged from the cries of joy and pain from their children's hearts.

He is not a Father who can only be rarely known, like earthly fathers who, whether by choice or reluctantly, only make contact with their children occasionally.

He is none of these.

He is the God and Father of our Lord Jesus Christ. You cannot separate the Father and the Son. The Father is the Father of Jesus. Jesus is the Son of the Father. Everything we know about the Father we know because of Jesus. He is just like Jesus.

He has fellowship with the fallen.

He has banquets with the broken.

He touches the untouchables.

He loves the unlovable.

He makes wine at weddings.

And he grieves at gravesides. As the psalmist proclaimed:

> You have stored my tears
> in your bottle
> and counted each of them.
> (Psalm 56.8 CEV)

This then is the perfect Father – the Father whose Son came on to our orphaned planet so that he could bring us home as his royally adopted sons and daughters. He is truly a Father to the fatherless and a champion for the orphan. He is relational, not remote. He believes in embrace, not exclusion.

Once you see God like this, you will gaze at the cross with marvelling eyes.

Like the prodigal, you will see him running towards you, his face wet with tears.

3

The passion of the Father

Sitting in a large cinema in London's Leicester Square with hundreds of film critics was a first for me. It was 2003; Mel Gibson's movie *The Passion of the Christ* was about to be released and I had been invited by the BBC to attend a press screening. The BBC wanted me to speak at a series of interviews a few days later on the Sunday morning, commenting on aspects of the movie. I was sometimes invited to discuss issues of faith and film, so I was looking forward to the challenge.

After a quick read of the press pack and a brief introduction from the film's producer, I sat back as the lights went down in the auditorium.

Nothing could have really prepared me for what followed. I had heard that the movie showed graphic depictions of Christ's sufferings. But this was beyond anything that I could have imagined. It was without doubt the most violent film I had ever watched. The torment of the seemingly endless flogging of Christ and then the lingering and minute focus on the process of crucifixion were almost too much to bear. I was not alone in shifting restlessly in my seat.

I'll be honest. At times I thought that Gibson's portrayal bordered on a glorification of pain. Other films of his such as *Apocalypto* don't hold back when it comes to bloodletting. *The Passion of the Christ* was so overwhelmingly brutal that after a while I found myself shutting down, as in other Gibson movies. This felt like a very angry film. Even the portrayal of God seemed to veer in this direction. Where was his love? Where was his forgiveness?

And then something unexpected happened.

At the moment when Jesus breathed his last breath (elongated and amplified on the soundtrack), the camera angle was elevated to a position far above the place of execution. As in Dalí's painting *Christ of St John of the Cross*, we were now afforded a vantage point above Golgotha.

At first I thought that the tiny figures way below were encased within a bubble. Then I realized, along with the hundreds of others in the cinema, that this was not a bubble but a raindrop – the first drop of a deluge.

As the contours of the raindrop became more defined, it seemed to detach itself from the tiny hill where the execution had just ended. Then it began to fall. Down, down it went, taking us with it, all the way from the darkening heavens to the dusty earth.

When it touched down in the stony sand at the foot of the cross, the splash seemed to be out of proportion to the size of the raindrop, and the sound felt more like that of a wave breaking than a drop of water landing.

Now it became clear.

It was more than a raindrop.

It was a tear – a divine tear.

Gibson was not showing us an angry God any more.

The Father was weeping over the death of his Son.

I wasn't alone in being affected by this evocative image. It was a singular and oddly discordant moment – a moment of tenderness during several hours of torture. Up until then, there had been little space given to the notion that God felt anything other than rage. And there wasn't afterwards either. For no sooner had the tear cascaded into the blood-soaked dust than a storm hit Calvary, and an earthquake devastated the Temple. It seemed that Mel Gibson couldn't resist reverting to the image of a raging God – the wind terrifying the Romans on the hill, and the earthquake reaping revenge on the Jewish leaders in the city.

But for several heartbeats the theology had changed as dramatically as the angle of vision. The Father's heart had been glimpsed.

Even if it was artistic licence, the picture of the falling tear was evocative. Gibson had gone from the explicit to the implicit, from the literal to the metaphorical, from the cruel to the kind. It is the stand-out moment in a film of horror and brutality.

The great hymnbook controversy

One of the reasons why the image of the teardrop moved me was because I had already begun to look at the cross from a different perspective. It had occurred to me that theologians had mostly focused on the Son's suffering at Calvary and on the benefits of that suffering for the believer. But what was the Father doing? What did he experience during the passion of his Son? What would happen if we focused on him?

This, in my view, is unexplored territory.

Often in the Western Church we have been told that the Father felt only one thing as his Son died: wrath. In a theory known as 'penal substitutionary atonement' (PSA), some theologians have proposed that the Father poured out his wrath upon his own Son at Golgotha. In this legal theory human beings stand guilty in the eyes of God, but the Son stands in our place and takes our punishment. We deserve to die because of our sinful rebellion against God. The penalty for such rebellion is death. But Christ graciously volunteers to take our place and suffers our punishment instead. God's wrath against sin is poured out upon the Son so that we can be freely pardoned. In this way Jesus' sufferings provide a 'satisfaction' for the Father's holy anger.[1]

This version of penal substitution, with the Father raging at his Son, has come in for heavy criticism.[2]

In the same year that I was commissioned to write this book, a controversy broke out over a couplet in a much loved contemporary hymn:

> Till on that cross as Jesus died,
> The wrath of God was satisfied.[3]

It all started when an American Presbyterian church committee decided to add 'In Christ Alone' to their new hymnbook, called *Glory to God*. Before they went to press, they decided to check with the authors of the hymn whether they could change the above lines to the following:

> Till on that cross as Jesus died,
> The love of God was magnified.

The two authors, Keith Getty and Stuart Townend, refused to grant permission for the changes, so the hymn in the end was withdrawn from the new collection.

What was the fuss about? When one of the committee members was asked, she replied that others were worried because the view 'that the cross is primarily about God's need to assuage God's anger' would be damaging to the worshipper's theological education.[4]

Needless to say, this response polarized people. On the one hand there were those who said we need hymns about God's wrath because otherwise we will end up sentimentalizing God's love. On the other hand there were equally strong voices arguing that the penal substitution theory is a grim invention of the medieval and Reformation imagination and should be jettisoned.

The latter viewpoint has caused outrage. For some people in the Church, believing in the doctrine of penal substitution has become the heart and soul of true Christianity. If you believe that Jesus satisfied the Father's wrath at Calvary, you're in. If you don't, you're out – along with the revised hymnbooks.

God's anger, God's love

I'm not likely to be able to make peace between these two polarized factions in a few paragraphs, but let me begin by saying this. The New Testament does indeed mention the wrath of God a number of times and there is no getting away from this. Having said that, we need to understand the term correctly if we are to make any headway.

What then is the wrath of God?

I define the wrath of God as *the Father's measured and justified anger over human sin, social injustice and demonic wickedness.* This at first sight seems paradoxical. God is love and yet there are things that he hates.

The Father hates it when people break his commandments, wilfully rejecting his offer of relationship, turning away from his gracious overtures of fatherly love.

The Father hates it when women and children are sold into slavery and then used and exploited as objects of sexual gratification.

The Father hates it when the enemy unleashes hell on families and even whole cultures, creating fatherless societies and orphaned hearts.

In the beauty of holiness, God hates such ugliness.

And surely this makes sense when we think about it. Do we truly believe that God doesn't long with an ardent intensity for the righting of great wrongs? Surely we have to believe that one day God will provide a higher justice for those who have been denied justice on earth. If not, then God may be full of love, but he is not just or good.[5]

The good news for the oppressed is that God's holy anger is being stored up against those who victimize the powerless and abuse the innocent. Seen in this light, God's wrath is an expression of his love – his love for those who are the victims of human abuse and demonic destruction.

Far from being a contradiction, therefore, God's love towards humankind and his hatred of wickedness are deeply interconnected and entirely compatible. God hates oppression because he loves the oppressed. He always has. If he had not, he would be loving, but not good.

The sin, not the Son

We cannot strip away the 'wrath of God' from the pages of the New Testament, nor can we remove anger completely from our picture of the divine love, not without in the process saying that in the end injustices are allowed to stand and vindication will be denied. Surely none of us in our right mind wants to believe that.

Yet at the same time, the idea that the Father poured out his anger on his Son at the cross, who somehow satisfied or slaked this righteous rage in his sacrificial death, needs to be rejected.

First of all, it needs to be rejected because it is in fact a caricature.[6] In reality, there is not just one view of penal substitution; there are several. The version that I have been describing is certainly one, but it is not necessarily the majority view, nor is it necessarily the biblical view. It is an extreme and exaggerated version of the truth.

Second, it has to be rejected because it actually distracts people from accepting a more nuanced view of penal substitution. In this more balanced and biblical view, it is not the Son who is the object of the Father's righteous rage at Calvary. It is human sin.

One passage that points to a punitive view of the death of Jesus can be found in Paul's Letter to the Romans. Some view Romans 3.23–26 as Paul's definitive description of Christ's death as penal substitution. There he writes:

> All have sinned and fall short of the glory of God, and all are justified freely by his grace through the redemption that came by Christ Jesus. God presented Christ as a sacrifice of atonement, through the shedding of his blood – to be received by faith. He did this to demonstrate his righteousness, because in his forbearance he had left the sins committed beforehand unpunished – he did it to demonstrate his righteousness at the present time, so as to be just and the one who justifies those who have faith in Jesus.

This is without doubt one of the great passages on the atoning death of Christ. But there is no reference here to the Son absorbing the wrath of the Father in his body on the cross. Those who use this passage to justify the view that the Father does violence to his Son have to import that idea from elsewhere. It is not in the passage itself, even though there is much about the wrath of God in Romans 1—3.

However, there is another passage in Romans that has a punitive nuance to it, Romans 8.3–4:

> What the law was powerless to do because it was weakened by the flesh, God did by sending his own Son in the likeness of sinful flesh to be a sin offering. And so he condemned sin in the flesh, in order that the righteous requirement of the law might be fully met in us, who do not live according to the flesh but according to the Spirit.

Here Paul talks about the extreme and disastrous power of sin in the human condition. It is sin that prevents us from fulfilling our calling to live as the righteous sons and daughters of God. In other words, sin debilitates us to such a degree that it is impossible for us to obey the Torah. Because of this, we forever open ourselves to the charge that we are lawbreakers and become painfully aware, through the accusations of the enemy, that we never measure up.

But, says Paul, God sent his Son to save us from this dreadful state. Christ identified completely with our human condition, becoming like us in our humanity while at the same time being quite unlike us in his purity. As such, the Son of God showed human beings what it means to be a son or a daughter of the high King of heaven. In sinful human flesh, Jesus lived a life of perfect sonship. Right to the last, he loved God with his entire being and his neighbour as himself.

When Christ went to the cross, he did for us what we couldn't do for ourselves. *He took the condemnation for sin – the condemnation found in God's Torah – in his dying human body.* In this way, Christ was our substitute. He did die a sacrificial death. And he also bore the condemnation that was rightfully ours. He did this so that we don't have to bear it.

But notice this.

God condemned *sin* in Christ's dying body.

He did not condemn his *Son*.

The rage that was burning in the heart of the Father was therefore not directed at his *Son* but at our *sin*. Between the words 'Son' and 'sin' there is a world of difference.

Distorting the Father

It seems to me there are two dangers at the moment when it comes to discussions about penal substitution. The first is that those who propose it are in grave danger of implying, and indeed sometimes stating, that this is the central metaphor of the atonement in the New Testament and that those who do not champion it in the way they do are not just in error; they are not even in Christ. This view is divisive.

The second danger is that those who reject it out of hand are at grave risk of rejecting just one version of it – an extreme version at that – when in fact there are more balanced and biblical versions that do not lead us to portray the Father as unleashing violent rage upon his Son.

In my view, it is entirely possible to hold a penal view of the atonement without resorting to the idea that the Son appeased the Father's wrath at Calvary. Apart from anything else, holding this extreme view of 'satisfaction' requires a distortion – I would say a mutilation – of our image of the Father. Sooner or later we have to ask, 'What kind of father treats his child in such a way?' And then, 'In what sense is this good news?'

If those outside the Church are presented with a message that requires them to believe that the Father is capable of such violently abusive actions, how will it ever be good news to them when stories of abusive fathers in our own social context are always bad news?

It could never be.[7]

One of the things I have experienced time and again as I have engaged in counselling and prayer ministry is the often heartbreaking sight of people being set free from the effects of abuse by their fathers. The critical moment in their liberation is always when they come to recognize in their hearts that their heavenly Father is not like their earthly father. *Abba* Father never shames them with words, with violence, emotional manipulation, suffocation, religious control or any other oppressive tactics. He is the exact opposite. Where abusive fathers shame, *Abba* Father honours. Where abusive fathers hurt, *Abba* Father heals.

What kind of good news is it, therefore, to the victim of paternal abuse that our Father in heaven poured out his wrath upon his Son at Calvary?

Is this kind of Father safe? Can this kind of Father be a source of freedom from the terrors of an abusive past? Is this kind of wrath in any sense a source of solace to the humiliated heart?

I would suggest that the answer has to be 'no'.

The image of the Father pouring out his wrath upon his one and only precious Son has to be vigorously questioned. Christ suffered in our place at the cross. That is a given. Christ's death is indeed sacrificial. That is also a given. But his death at Calvary did not involve him appeasing or satisfying the Father's wrath. If it did, then Jesus ends up saving us from the Father as much as from sin. To say that would mean dividing the Trinity into a bad-cop/good-cop dynamic – the Father being against us, the Son being for us.

A grief observed

If the Father was not feeling wrath towards his Son at Calvary, then what was he feeling?

In some people's minds this question shouldn't be asked at all. 'God does not feel as we feel. Even his wrath is more of a state of mind than what we would call a feeling. What you're doing is projecting human emotions onto God. You're guilty of anthropo-morphizing God the Father.'[8]

If you believe this, please keep in mind that we are all created in the image of God, and if that is so, then our human emotions are reflections – however distorted – of divine affections. We cannot therefore so easily dismiss the existence of divine feelings. God truly does experience what we would term 'emotions'. They may be different from ours in terms of their perfection, but that doesn't mean that they bear no generic likeness to what we experience.

God the Father feels for us, not just as a state of mind, but with his heart. He relates to us affectively, not just cognitively. Do we really think that when the Scriptures talk about the Father rejoicing over his people with singing (Zephaniah 3.17) this is purely a state of mind? Have we not moved beyond our idolatry of reason and our suspicion of emotion? Surely it is time to embrace the idea that *Abba* Father has feelings towards his Son and indeed towards us.

What, then, was the Father's experience as he gazed upon his dying Son? If it wasn't divine rage, what was it?

The answer cannot be summed up adequately in a few words. Even the wisest philosopher or the most lyrical of poets would find it impossible to do justice in language to the Father's experience at Calvary.

What we can say is that what happened at the cross embraced the whole of the Trinity. While the three persons of the Godhead are inseparable – three in one and one in three – they did experience the same Calvary event individually. What the Father experienced was accordingly different from what the Son experienced, and what the Father felt was the very worst kind of grief – the agonizing sorrow of seeing his own Son die.

There are few agonies more appalling than the sight of one's own child in pain, in peril and at the point of death. One of the greatest tragedies of all is when parents have to confront the fact they are going to outlive their own child. It is a gut-wrenching sadness, the most inexplicable mystery. In my decades as a parish priest the most harrowing moments were those in which I had to minister to a dying child and then oversee his or her funeral, in the company of the distraught parents and family. There is no apparent sense in this and it is very hard to explain to the bereaved why such things happen. There is no theodicy that I have ever encountered that offers a completely satisfying explanation why such desolate moments have to be endured. It is utterly perplexing and deeply devastating. As King Theoden says in the second *Lord of the Rings* movie, 'No parent should have to bury their child.'

But if they do, there is one crumb of comfort and it is this. Our Father has endured the same pain. He too has watched in unutterable distress as his Son suffered and then died. He too has stood and wept with those who mourn. He too has seen his Son buried. In that, there is at least some solace.

When Jesus made his cry of desolation from the cross, he used words from the beginning of Psalm 22. Later on in that same psalm King David says this of God's response to the afflictions of his servant:

> For he has not despised or scorned
>   the suffering of the afflicted one;
> he has not hidden his face from him
>   but has listened to his cry for help.
> (Psalm 22.24)

What was true for the Son by nature is true for the sons and daughters by adoption. The Father doesn't turn his heart away from us when we suffer. He turns his face towards us, not away, and he is not deaf to our cries but truly attentive.

Abba Father is not apathetic. He does not hide his face from our tears.

Losing contact

There is one more thing to say.

When the sin of the world was absorbed into Jesus' dying body, there was a breach in the Son's experience of his relationship with his Father.

This was inevitable. God is holy. When Christ, who never sinned, took the sin of the world in his human flesh, there was a momentary separation between the Father and the Son. This was not because the Father stopped loving his Son. It was because the world's sin created a barrier between the Father and the Son and between the Son and his Father. Sin does that. It separates and divides families and peoples. We will look later at what this must have felt like from the Son's side, but from the Father's perspective it must have grieved him in ways we can only begin to imagine.

While the Trinity was not fractured (and can never be fractured), in those moments when the Son became sin for our sakes there had to have been great sorrow. The Father still adored his Son, but our sin made it impossible for the two to dwell together in that same holy intimacy that they had always enjoyed.

Our sin divided *Abba* from his only Son for the one and only time from eternity to eternity.

How did the sun not fall from the sky?

One of the most excruciating experiences that a father can endure is loss of contact with his children. This can happen for many reasons, but when it does, a father's heart breaks.

And here I have to be honest. I have just endured a terrible year. As a result of my own weakness, I have lost contact with my four children. Whereas before I was able to be with them most of the time, now I do not see them at all. Where there was once constant communication, whether written or spoken, now there is nothing.

I cannot begin to put into words the agony I feel because of this. It is my sin that has created the barrier, not theirs. But I pine for my children night and day, longing for just one phone call, one letter, one email, one text – anything.

The only thing that helps me in my distress is the consoling thought that my Father in heaven understands. Even if it is true that in his case he was sinless (whereas in mine I am not), I know that he knows. He has been there. At Calvary he endured separation from his Son. I can lean my head on his grieving heart and find comfort there.

He understands.

Back to the movies

So I return to where I began this chapter, with *The Passion of the Christ*.

It may be that I was a little hard on Mel Gibson's film. I know of at least one life that was changed as a result of it, that of my twin sister Claire. She had been on a long journey of spiritual seeking when she found her way into a multiplex cinema in the state of New Mexico where she lives. Seeing on the screen what Jesus had endured for her, she surrendered. All her resistance to the divine love gave in. She opened her heart to the Love of all loves and is now a committed Christian, serving the Lord and growing from strength to strength in her faith in Christ.

So perhaps I was harsh. I was moved by the film too, at least when the Father's tear fell from heaven onto the soil of Golgotha. Gibson, for all his faults, had seen something. He had not only seen the passion of the Son. He had connected with the passion of the Father.

In that passion there is hope for all those who grieve at the loss of intimacy, and even relationship, with their own children.

In that compassion there is healing.

4

A story of adoption

It was one of the most surreal moments of my life. I was sitting with five companions on plastic chairs on the green grass of a garden overlooking the vibrant Ugandan city of Kampala. We were sheltered from the blistering sun in a small marquee whose canvas twitched at the intrusions of an unlikely breeze. The tent had been set up in the burgeoning grounds of one of the five royal palaces belonging to the king of the largest tribe in the nation. The eight of us in the delegation were sitting in two rows facing each other. The king was seated to my right in an upholstered armchair that was resting on the grass. He looked relaxed in his short-sleeved summer shirt as he prepared to receive us.

It was my mother who put me up to it when she heard that I was going to Uganda to visit an orphanage that had based its curriculum on my book, *From Orphans to Heirs*.

'Why don't you write to the king? He might be able to see you.'

'He won't have time for me,' I had replied.

'He was in your father's house at Bradfield College,' Mum continued. 'He'll remember you, even though you were only about six or seven when he was there as one of Dad's pupils. I'm sure he'd love to meet you. Just post a letter to the Ugandan Embassy and see what happens.'

And so I did. The letter went off and the king replied almost immediately, saying he would love to meet on the Sunday of my visit. When he heard that my purpose was to visit an orphanage, he asked me to bring its leaders with me.

'I remember your father well,' the king remarked underneath the sun-bleached awning, before launching into his own memoirs of my dad's many kindnesses to him. 'When my father was assassinated,' he said, 'your father stepped in and took care of me.'

From that moment on, my dad had watched over the fatherless prince in the boarding house where he was housemaster. Later he helped him to land a place at university. When President Idi Amin – Uganda's dictator – was finally exiled to Saudi Arabia, the call went out to find the African prince in England. Once he had been discovered, he returned to his country to be crowned king, to the great joy of many.

The king invited my father to attend the much publicized coronation. When Dad came back afterwards, he had a suntan and arms full of bows, arrows, drums and small statues of African warriors, which he gave to the three of us children. I had been mesmerized.

'Your father was an extraordinary man,' the king mused, one hour after he had started the conversation.

'He was truly a father to the fatherless,' I said. 'Many boys who are now grown adults – some now in their sixties – have told me how he looked after them when their own father died, even paying the school fees for some of them when they fell on hard times.'

A few moments later the topic turned seamlessly to the other members of the delegation and our Christian faith. The king was fascinated as we shared our stories with him. It seemed that the subject of my own father had created a perfect platform for talking about our Father in heaven.

We were allocated 20 minutes, but it was after two and a half hours that the audience came to an end.

'Would you mind if I prayed for you?' I asked the king.

'Not at all,' he replied. He stood to attention, bowing his head reverently, closing his eyes.

I stood next to him and laid a hand on his shoulder, after asking his permission. 'Heavenly Father, I thank you,' I whispered, 'that both the king and I have had the privilege of being loved and looked after by an amazing father. But the truth is that your Son Jesus has revealed to us that you too are a Father to the fatherless.

In fact, you are the perfect Father. Would you show the king that you are his Father and would you bless him with your kindness, in Christ's name. Amen.'

The king slowly opened his eyes. He had obviously been deeply touched.

He shook my hand firmly and gratefully. I gave him a hardback version of my book *The Father You've Been Waiting For*, and he promised me that he would place it by his bed and read it avidly.[1]

And with that, my friends and I left the tent and the garden and proceeded back through the slums to the orphanage, whose good work was now known to the king. Later he was to conduct a royal visit there and thank the leaders and the workers for caring for his nation's fatherless children.

A Father to the fatherless

I wrote in the opening chapter of this book that I owe so much to my adoptive father, not least because he demonstrated in his own character and actions something of the limitless contours of the divine Father's love.

Dad and Mum had gone to great lengths to adopt Claire and me and bring us home. Thanks to them, although we had been orphans, we now became their son and daughter. We had been impoverished and hopeless, but our lives were now rich in undeserved opportunities.

In all of this, Dad played a pivotal role. He truly was a father to the fatherless, not just to Claire and me, but also to those pupils who found themselves without parents during their time in my father's house. Taking care of the fatherless was his passion. Is it any wonder, then, given this background, that I cannot help seeing the God and Father of the Bible as an adopting Father?

This picture of God's character is not just displayed in the New Testament (as we will see later); it is in the Old Testament too. In fact, it is often forgotten that throughout the Hebrew Scriptures God is portrayed as the Father whose heart goes out in fervent love towards the fatherless and who requires his leaders and his people to take care of those who become orphans and widows. Israel and Judah are therefore consistently challenged to love the fatherless. Their kings are to provide practical support for them. Those who do not are roundly condemned by the prophets.

King David heard and obeyed this commission to promote the cause of the orphan. In Psalm 68 he says:

> A father to the fatherless, a defender of widows,
>   is God in his holy dwelling.
> God sets the lonely in families,
>   he leads out the prisoners with singing;
>   but the rebellious live in a sun-scorched land.
> (verses 5–6)

Notice the evocative title given to God Almighty here. He is 'a father to the fatherless'. His divine presence in his 'holy dwelling' is a fatherly presence. It is the presence of the one who longs to gather up street children and lost orphans into his tender arms. This presence is accordingly not only the radiant light of God's holy and majestic glory. It is also the manifestation of the Love of all loves – the love that enfolds the grieving widow and the traumatized child in an all-powerful but gentle embrace.

Here it is worth remembering that King David practised what he proclaimed. When his friend Jonathan died, he left a son called Mephibosheth. Mephibosheth was just five years old when he lost both his father Jonathan and his grandfather Saul. As he was fleeing from the palace with his nurse, Mephibosheth had an accident and tragically became lame in both legs. He was taken to Lo-Debar – a place whose very name denotes loneliness and barrenness – where he spent the next 15 years.

Then one day King David woke up and thought to himself, 'Is there anyone left in Saul's family to whom I can show kindness for Jonathan's sake?' (2 Samuel 9.1 GW). After making enquiries, David heard about Mephibosheth and had his servants send for the now 20-year-old son of Jonathan.

When Mephibosheth arrived, David said this: 'Don't be afraid, for I will surely show you kindness for the sake of your father Jonathan. I will restore to you all the land that belonged to your grandfather Saul, and you will always eat at my table' (2 Samuel 9.7).

As an orphan, Mephibosheth had been living in fear, but now the king was showing him love.

He had been cruelly treated, but now he was being visited by kindness.

He had been robbed of all his inheritance, but now he was receiving a great restoration.

He had become used to eating scraps, but now he was going to feast at the king's table.

He had come to regard himself as an orphan, but now he was going to live as a prince.

All this, thanks to David's kindness.

What is this if it is not the Father's heart expressed through Israel's greatest king? No wonder God called David 'a man after his own heart' (1 Samuel 13.14). David himself acted as a father to the fatherless. He set a lonely man in a family – his own family. If that isn't the adopting heart of Father God, I don't know what is.

God's covenant love

The story of Mephibosheth is not just a cameo of David's royal compassion. It is more important than that; it is actually a microcosm of the big story of the Hebrew Bible. All this is suggested by the simple word 'kindness'.

The episode begins with David asking himself if there is anyone in Saul's family to whom he can show 'kindness'. When David eventually meets Saul's orphaned grandson, he reassures him by saying, 'I will surely show you kindness.'

In the original Hebrew language the word translated 'kindness' is *hesed*. This is a technical term in the Old Testament. It is frequently used of the commitment of God to go on and on loving his people because of the covenant he has made with them. It is a word that points to his choice to adopt Israel as his own and to love its people, come what may.

God is characterized by two things in this covenant relationship: *hesed* and *hemet*. The first word denotes the loving kindness and persistent love of God, the second his faithfulness to his people and to his promises. Both of these are vital covenant qualities.

When David wakes up one morning with the word 'kindness' (*hesed*) on his lips, he is effectively referring to covenant love – to the 'love that will not let the other person go'. David and Jonathan had formed a covenant. Now the king is showing his loving kindness (*hesed*) towards Jonathan's son, and his faithfulness (*hemet*) to his and Jonathan's promises.

In adopting the 20-year-old orphan into his family, inviting him to feast daily at his table, David takes the boy from a life of servitude to a life of sonship, from a life of being the tail to a life of being the head. In this respect, David's behaviour is a picture in miniature of the adopting heart of God. In the Old Testament, what David did for Mephibosheth is what the Father did for Israel.

All this shows how the unimposing story of Mephibosheth, whose name means 'shattered shame', acts as a microcosm of the larger story of the Father's love for his own people. David shows *hesed* in adopting an orphaned exile, all within the overarching narrative of God's kind act of adopting Israel.

The big story

It should never, therefore, be forgotten that the Hebrew Bible, taken as a whole, is in fact a poignant story of national adoption. Out of his great love for this orphaned planet, the Father begins the process of redemption and reconciliation by choosing one nation out of all the nations of the world. This is an extraordinary choice.

God could have chosen the Egyptians with their monumental pyramids and palaces.

He could have chosen the Greeks with their abiding legacy of wisdom and learning.

He could have chosen the Romans with their heroic leaders and terrifying armies.

But he did not.

When the Father adopted a nation, he chose the small, not the great; the ordinary, not the extraordinary; the weak, not the strong. That is why, while all the other empires and powers have risen and fallen, come and gone, the nation of Israel has remained, often against all the odds.

When God chose to make a covenant with Israel this was permanent, not transient. In God's eyes, adoption is forever.

So it is that we see God the Father pouring out his love upon a band of nomads in the desert, not because of any merit on their part, but because he simply looked upon them and loved them. As Moses says, 'The LORD your God has chosen you out of all the peoples of the face of the earth to be his people, his treasured possession' (Deuteronomy 7.6).

Why did God choose to adopt Israel? Had Israel earned the right to become his 'treasured possession?' Moses answers the question in the next two verses:

> The LORD did not set his affection on you and choose you because you were more numerous than other peoples, for you were the fewest of all peoples. But it was because the LORD loved you and kept the oath he swore to your ancestors that he brought you out with a mighty hand and redeemed you from the land of slavery, from the power of Pharaoh king of Egypt.   (Deuteronomy 7.7–8)

Here we have it. God did not choose the people of Israel because they were moral or mighty. He chose them because he had chosen to love them, and this devotion was one with a history. He had made promises to their ancestors. He had formed a covenant long before with Abraham.

Here we see the virtues of *hesed* and *hemet* once again. The Father's love for Israel was a steadfast, persevering, continuing love. It was a kindness and affection without a sell-by date. That's *hesed*. As such, he wasn't going to give up on them. He was going to remain faithful even when they were not. That's *hemet*. God's affection for Israel was therefore more than a warm feeling; it was a costly commitment.

The end of slavery

The Hebrew Bible teaches at a number of points that the journey out of Egypt was the formalizing of Israel's adoption as a nation.

When Moses – an orphaned child, adopted as a royal son – is called to be the deliverer of Israel, he is told to go and tell Pharaoh that Israel is his firstborn son and that he is to let God's son go (Exodus 4.22–23).

Notice here what the God of the universe calls the oppressed Hebrew slaves in Egypt: 'my firstborn son'. The word 'firstborn' should not be taken literally, referring to Israel's genetic status. Rather it should be understood figuratively, as referring to that nation's privileged position. In Hebrew culture, the firstborn son was the honoured son, the one granted the double portion of his father's inheritance. This is Israel's joy. Adopted by the God of the universe, Israel enjoys the double portion over all other nations, with an inheritance greater than that of any other people.

So it is that the Father raises up an orphaned boy called Moses and commands him to go to the king of Egypt to tell him to release the Hebrew slaves. Pharaoh refuses until after the tenth plague, when he momentarily relents and the exodus of the Israelites begins. With that, the Israelites take the first steps of a journey that is not just physical but also spiritual. It is a journey through the desert to the land of promise, yes. But it is also a journey into the fullness of their adopted, national sonship. This is why God will later say of the exodus, 'out of Egypt I called my son' (Hosea 11.1). Their liberation was not just salvation *from* something. It was salvation *to* something. It was a transition from slavery to sonship.

The Hebrew Bible therefore tells a story of adoption. The story of Moses, in which an orphaned slave becomes a royally adopted son, is a microcosm of the story of Israel.

The gift of intimacy

The primary purpose of the Father's adoption of Israel was relational before anything else. He chose to rescue the Hebrew slaves so that they could have the freedom to worship him. This lifestyle of worship was not to be dry, formal and lifeless. It was to be deeply personal, loving and heartfelt. In short, God wanted his adopted son to be emancipated so that the two could enjoy a friendship that was not possible while the Israelites were bowed down under the heavy yoke of an enslaving father, namely Pharaoh. In short, God the Father was after intimacy with his liberated son.

Listen to what is said when the covenant between the Father and his adopted national son is about to be ratified at Mount Sinai:

> Then Moses went up to God, and the LORD called to him from the mountain and said, 'This is what you are to say to the descendants of Jacob and what you are to tell the people of Israel: "You yourselves have seen what I did to Egypt, and how I carried you on eagles' wings and brought you to myself. Now if you obey me fully and keep my covenant, then out of all nations you will be my treasured possession. Although the whole earth is mine, you will be for me a kingdom of priests and a holy nation."'   (Exodus 19.3–6)

Here God outlines the contours of the covenant: 'You obey what I require of you in my covenant and you will be a kingdom of priests, a holy nation.'

What is this blessing of priesthood?

When we think of the word 'priest' we may mistakenly think of someone who represents formal religion. But this is not at all what is meant by the word in this context. The Hebrew word is *cohen*, which means 'one who draws near'. A priest in this context is therefore the very opposite of someone who has a religious rather than a relational knowledge of God. A priest in this sense means one who is privileged to draw near to the God who is transcendent and holy. A priest is a person who has learned to excel in intimacy. Living a life of obedience, she or he revels in God's friendship. To use the exquisite words of Sarah Edwards, such a person enjoys a sense of God's 'nearness to me, my dearness to him'.[2]

This was the purpose of the covenant of adoption, formalized at Mount Sinai. The Israelites were called to live as the true representatives of their adopting Father. The commandments described what the ethics of sonship entailed: living in a way that showed they loved God with all their heart, mind, soul and strength, and their neighbour as themselves. These were the Father's instructions. As such, the laws that made up the Torah were never meant to be understood as the conditions of a legal contract. They were meant to be the teaching of a loving Father – teaching designed not to punish but to protect, not to curse but to bless. If the Israelites kept the covenant, then they would all enjoy priestly intimacy with God.

Here then is the purpose of the covenant – the adoption agreement – between God and the nation of Israel. If the people heard and obeyed his commandments, then they would continually live as a kingdom of *cohanim*, a nation of royal intimates of the loving God of the universe.

The people of Israel were therefore called to enjoy the Lord's intimate presence. This presence is called *panim* in Hebrew, which can be translated 'face'. When God called his people to become priests, he was calling them to dwell in the light of his smile. If the people lived lives befitting God's adopted son, then like Moses they would encounter God's manifested presence, and their faces would become luminous (Exodus 33.11; Numbers 6.22–27).

See how the love of the Father radiates from all of this. God loves his people as a father loves his son. As Moses declares in Deuteronomy 1.31: 'You saw how the LORD your God carried you, as a father carries his son, all the way you went'.

Theirs is the adoption

So we return finally to the wonderful kindness of God. This kindness is undeserved. It is right at the very heart of the big story of the Old Testament, which is a story of unmerited, loving, national adoption.

It is thus critical to remember that it is not just in the New Testament that God displays adopting grace. This adopting grace is clearly visible in the Old Testament too. Indeed, in the mind of the apostle Paul adoption was the greatest gift given to Israel:

> Theirs is the adoption to sonship; theirs the divine glory, the covenants, the receiving of the law, the temple worship and the promises. Theirs are the patriarchs, and from them is traced the human ancestry of the Messiah, who is God over all, for ever praised! Amen. (Romans 9.4–5)

Notice the order in which Paul lists the unique blessings bestowed on his own race, by which he means 'the people of Israel':

the adoption to sonship;
the divine glory;
the covenants;
the receiving of the Torah;
the Temple worship;
the promises;
the patriarchs;
the Messiah's ancestry.

The first item in the list of Israel's privileges is Israel's adoption to sonship. Even more important than the *shekinah* glory of God, Israel's adoption is revered and hallowed by the apostle Paul. Out of Israel's many exceptional privileges, he chooses the kindness of God in adopting Israel as number one in the catalogue of covenant blessings. If that adoption had not taken place, there would have been no one to see the manifestation of God's glory, to receive the covenants and promises, to engage in the Temple and its worship, to learn from the patriarchs and the Messiah Jesus himself.

Do you see how central the idea of adoption is to the great story of the people of Israel? Before any of us were adopted individually by the Father, Israel was adopted nationally. Indeed, if Israel had not been adopted, there would have been no family from whom the Son of God could be born. Without the birth of the Son of God, there would have been no adoption of the sons and daughters of God.

The adoption of Israel therefore opens up the fatherly heart of God to us. It reveals the glorious truth that God is supremely our Strong Deliverer, the one who leads us out of the misery of slavery to the ecstasy of sonship.

God is, and has always been, into adoption. This was the primary reason for the Incarnation, the birth of God's Son. It was the primary reason why the Son of God voluntarily chose to die for this orphaned planet.

The biblical story is truly a metanarrative of adoption.

5

The orphaned angel

———•◦•———

It has often been said that it was easier to get the Israelites out of Egypt than to get Egypt out of the Israelites. This is the tragedy of Israel's Old Testament history. Called as a nation to the lofty heights of royal adoption, Israel gravitated back towards the desperate slavery from which it had been so gloriously rescued.

This was true in the period of the kingdom of Israel before it divided. It was true afterwards, in both the history of Israel (the northern kingdom) and the history of Judah (the southern kingdom). No matter how much the prophets pleaded, it seemed that God's people never lost the rebellious strain that so often characterizes and debilitates the orphan heart. They continually fell into collective sin, breaking the Father's commandments and in the process choosing slavery over sonship, oppression over liberation.

In the last chapter I quoted God's words at the beginning of Hosea 11: 'out of Egypt I called my son.' Those words are part of a lament in which the Father weeps over the unfaithfulness of the nation he adopted:

> When Israel was a child, I loved him,
>   and out of Egypt I called my son.
> But the more they were called,
>   the more they went away from me.
> They sacrificed to the Baals
>   and they burned incense to images.
>   (Hosea 11.1–2)

51

Here we hear the poignant cry of a father who adopted a son, and gave him love and protection, only to see that son rebel against his love, as the prodigal did in Luke 15.

See how the lament continues:

> It was I who taught Ephraim to walk,
>   taking them by the arms;
> but they did not realise
>   it was I who healed them.
> I led them with cords of human kindness,
>   with ties of love.
> To them I was like one who lifts
>   a little child to the cheek,
>   and I bent down to feed them.
>   (Hosea 11.3–4)

Israel's God speaks here as a doting, adoptive father who taught his little boy how to walk, whisked him up in his arms, lifted him to his face, healed him when he was injured, and bent down to give him food. This is love!

But Israel rejected this fatherly love. Both after entering the promised land and after the division of the kingdoms, God's people chose behaviour that led them out of sonship back into slavery. Instead of choosing to be led by cords of love, they chose to be driven by whips.

And every time they did, it broke their Father's heart.

The morning star

This leads to an unavoidable question: why did God's people behave this way? Why, after receiving the privileged status of being God's adopted son, and the gift of God's presence, did they behave unfaithfully and ungratefully? Was it a case of poor human choices? Or was there something more sinister at work?

We cannot avoid the fact that God's people broke the commandments during the periods of history prior to the coming of God's

Son. Destructive choices were made, and not just occasionally. There were seasons in Old Testament history when the people of God were not faithful to the covenant promises. Having been warned that disobedience would cause God's blessings to be removed, they still chose to sacrifice to other gods and to burn incense to images. Called to be a son, Israel behaved like an orphan.

At the same time, we cannot put all this down to human choices alone. There were other factors involved. In particular, there were spiritual powers operating in the cosmos that were hell-bent on leading Israel back into slavery. These demonic powers worked to seduce God's people away from the abundant life of obedient sonship into the oppressive and impoverished life of the orphan condition.

What were these dark powers?

It is here that we enter a realm that will appear to some more akin to mythology than history. The Bible portrays a world in which light and darkness have been at war since the beginning. Many Jewish and Christian theologians agree that this war was triggered by the rebellion of one of heaven's angels during primordial time – an angel by the name of Lucifer.

It is often forgotten that 'Lucifer' is not a malevolent name in itself. In fact, the name Lucifer means 'light bringer' and is the Latin translation of the Hebrew word *heylel* in Isaiah 14.12, meaning 'morning star'. In the Greek translation (the Septuagint) the word in Isaiah 14.12 is *heosphoros*, 'bringer of dawn'. This is a word with a positive, not a negative, connotation.

According to Jewish and Christian theological traditions, Lucifer was therefore originally an angel – a created celestial being called to serve and worship God. However, something caused this shining one to rebel against the Father's love. According to the first and second books of *Enoch* – volumes written by a group in Judaism between the Old and the New Testaments – it was the creation of Adam that caused the heart of Lucifer to turn from God. When he was commanded by God to give reverence to Adam, the angel refused. Thus pride towards God was added to envy towards humanity, and Lucifer's fate was sealed.

Falling from heaven

During the time between the Testaments, pre-Christian groups (such as the one that produced *1* and *2 Enoch*) began to interpret Isaiah 14.12–15 as referring to Lucifer:

> How you have fallen from heaven,
> morning star, son of the dawn!
> You have been cast down to the earth,
> you who once laid low the nations!
> You said in your heart,
> 'I will ascend to the heavens;
> I will raise my throne
> above the stars of God;
> I will sit enthroned on the mount of assembly,
> on the utmost heights of Mount Zaphon.
> I will ascend above the tops of the clouds;
> I will make myself like the Most High.'
> But you are brought down to the realm of the dead,
> to the depths of the pit.

Although Isaiah 14.12–15 alluded in its original context to the hubris and ruination of a king of Babylon, Jewish and Christian interpreters understood it also to refer to Lucifer. Some of the fathers of the early Church followed suit. There is thus precedent for saying that these verses refer *simultaneously* to the fall of an historical king and to the prehistorical fall of Lucifer.

So what happened? According to Isaiah 14, an angel called to worship God decided to rebel. Origen, Chrysostom, Jerome, Ambrose and Augustine attributed this rebellion to pride towards God. Irenaeus, Justin Martyr, Cyprian and Tertullian put it down to envy towards human beings.

In his prelapsarian state (that is, before his fall), Lucifer had been focused on conforming his will to God's will. Angels are created beings, albeit celestial ones, and as such they have free will. But when his heart began to grow proud and envious, Lucifer changed from obeying God's will to wanting to satisfy his own will. The five 'I will' statements in this passage provide tragic evidence:

I will ascend to the heavens;
I will raise my throne;
I will sit enthroned;
I will ascend above the tops of the clouds;
I will make myself like the Most High.

Thanks to these orphan-hearted choices, Lucifer is now cast down from heaven to earth. He is hurled down to the realm of the dead, to the depths of the pit. Having lived in the radiant glory of heaven, the 'realm of the dead' is now his home.

This appalling judgement was one Lucifer brought upon himself. His self-inflicted fate was the worst imaginable. When he was cast out of heaven, Lucifer was expelled from the immediate presence of the Father's love. Nothing could be worse than that.

If going to hell means being separated by one's own choices from the kind and faithful love of the Father, then Lucifer's fall was into the very depths of hell. It is to this moment that Jesus referred after the return of the 70 disciples when he said, 'I saw Satan fall like lightning from heaven' (Luke 10.18).

Notice the change of name here. Lucifer has become 'Satan'. The bearer of the dawn, the star of the morning, the radiant one has become the 'adversary' (the literal translation of *ha satan*, Satan).

Satan is accordingly the orphaned angel, and those angels who followed him, and who fell with him from heaven, are orphaned angels too.

The orphan's revenge

The biblical story teaches that the war between light and darkness in our cosmos is a real war and a war waged by the original orphan against the triune God.

Although this war began in heaven, Satan soon turned planet earth into his battlefield. Lacking the power and authority to conduct his campaign of hatred and revenge in the heavenly realms, he infiltrated the Garden of Eden to go on the offensive on earth instead. His target was Adam, whose name can be translated as 'humankind'.

It is important at this point to remember that Adam was called to two great privileges. The first was the privilege of intimacy. Adam was created to be God's son, relating to God as his Father. This is clear from a detail in the genealogy of Jesus in the Gospel of Luke – a detail that can often be overlooked. When Luke describes the family history of Jesus the Messiah, he doesn't go back to Abraham, as Matthew does in his Gospel; he goes right back to Adam. When he comes to Adam he describes him as 'the son of God' (Luke 3.38).

When God created Adam he created him for a filial relationship. He made humankind in love and for love. His longing was to relate to Adam as a son and for Adam to relate to him as his Father. Adam's original identity was therefore not defined by his work in the garden or his task on the earth, but rather by his standing or position in relation to God. He was created to be a son, and Eve was created to be a daughter. The greatest privilege given to our first human parents was thus one of relating intimately to the triune God.

This honour should never be underestimated. The triune God created the stars, the universe and the earth as a home perfectly fashioned and gloriously fine-tuned for his son and daughter. When God created the heavens and the earth, he spoke them into being. 'Let there be light,' the Word exclaims (Genesis 1.3). And there was light. But when it came to Adam, God formed him with his own loving hands. And when he had formed Adam, he filled him with his *ruach*, his breath of life.

The first thing the wakening Adam therefore saw was the joyful countenance of his heavenly Father.

Adam's first experience was face-to-face intimacy with *Abba* Father.

If the first privilege given to Adam and Eve was one of relating, the second was one of ruling. They were commanded to have children and to go into the whole earth, bringing God's dominion to every part of God's Creation. This means that the *shalom* of Eden was meant to be brought to the rest of the planet. The earth as a whole did not yet enjoy the same order, harmony and beauty of Eden. Adam and Eve were mandated to bring the planet under the rule of their loving Father. They were called to bring heaven to earth.

The two privileges and priorities of our first parents can therefore be summed up in the words 'sonship' and 'kingship'. They were to have the identity of a son and a daughter, and the authority of a king and a queen.

It should come as no surprise, then, that Satan, masquerading as a talking serpent, should enter Eden with one purpose: to turn our first parents from a son and a daughter into orphans. This was what had happened to him. He was and is the original orphan. Having entered the orphan state, his vindictive plan was to seduce Eve and then Adam into forsaking their filial relationship with God. Having become separated from the Father's love, Satan worked to lure Eve and then Adam into becoming separated from that same love as well.

This was his strategy. It has always been his strategy. And as the apostle Paul warned, we should not be ignorant of the devil's schemes (2 Corinthians 2.9–11).

The human condition

Tragically, Eve and then Adam yielded to the orphan-maker's enchantment, and fell from being a daughter and a son who reign in love to being orphans who hide in fear. This hubris, this fall from grace, is the tragedy of all tragedies. And it had catastrophic effects.

If the plight of the orphan is primarily defined in terms of separation from the Father's love, then that is an apt description of the legacy of the First Adam. Whether you see Genesis 1—3 as history or myth, these chapters point to the universal human problem. We are by nature far away from the Father's love, and if we relate to God at all it is not as relational sons and daughters but as driven, religious slaves. As such, we languish in the toxic legacy of our first parents and we live outside Eden, in a disordered world, longing for reconnection with the Love of all loves.

Thanks to Eve and Adam, then, we are all spiritual orphans by nature. As the apostle Paul put it in Romans 5.12: 'sin entered the world through one man, and death through sin, and in this way death came to all people, because all sinned.'

Thus the orphan virus has infected all of us. Our instinctive reflex is to sin as Adam and Eve sinned, and indeed as Lucifer sinned. In other words, it seems like our default setting is to rebel against the Father's love and to live as spiritual orphans, far away from the Father's house. However much we want to restore the factory settings, we cannot erase through our own efforts the Adamic virus that eats away at the hard drive of our nature. In spite of our best efforts, we cannot mask the primal wound of separation through either work or play. Deep down within our orphaned hearts we look wistfully over our shoulders at the bolted gates of Eden.

Over time there have been many attempts to describe the effects of Adam's ancestral sin. Most have tended to focus on the subject of guilt, suggesting that human beings share in the consequences of what Eve and then Adam did. For some writers the effects of what Adam did have been small. In their view the Adamic legacy is slight. We have a tendency towards sin, but there is no collective guilt. At the other end of the spectrum there are those who say that the effects have been disastrous. Human beings are all guilty because we are all of us totally depraved on account of the First Adam's sin.

This focus on guilt has tended to distract us from the equally important subject of shame. Adam's separation from the Father's love brought shame into his life. That is why he hides. It is why he is afraid. It is also why he tries to cover his nakedness. This is shame, and this shame goes hand in hand with his sense of separation.

But this shame is not confined to Eve and Adam. It affects every human being. We do not naturally feel honoured. We do not inherently feel that we are princesses or princes. Separated from the affirming love of our heavenly Father, we do not merely feel alienated; we feel ashamed. We feel as if we have no merit, no value, no worth, in and of ourselves.

This is the agony of the human condition. Created for communion with our Father, we lack intimacy with the triune God and therefore lack the knowledge of who we are and how greatly we are loved. Every effort on our part to mask this shame fails dismally, and thus we fall far short of fulfilling our destiny to become the much-loved children of God.

This predicament ultimately comes from Satan, who revels in turning sons and daughters into orphans and slaves.

The slave-driver

This then is the enemy's primary tactic: to create orphans and slaves. He is supremely the orphan-maker – the one who seeks to keep people in a state of orphan-hearted slavery. So what does this slavery look like?

John Wesley, in his frequent preaching on our adoption in Christ, distinguished between two types of slavery. He described first of all the 'natural' person, the man or woman who by nature is drawn into slavery to sin. People in this state, Wesley says, think that they are free. But in reality they are slaves. As Wesley puts it in his sermon on 'The Spirit of Bondage and of Adoption':[1]

[This person] remains a willing servant of sin, content with the bondage of corruption . . . Such is the state of every natural man; whether he be a gross, scandalous transgressor, or a more reputable and decent sinner, having the form, though not the power of godliness.

59

But then there is the second kind of slavery, to the law. This type of person Wesley describes as 'the legal man'. Having been awakened from their sleepy state of ignorance, 'natural' individuals now feel condemned by God's law. Like slaves, they strive to become good enough, to measure up to the high standards of God, but to no avail. Satan still holds them fast in his chains. As Wesley poignantly observes:

> But though he strive with all his might, [the 'legal' person] cannot conquer: Sin is mightier than he. He would fain escape; but he is so fast in prison, that he cannot get forth. He is resolved against sin, but yet sins on: He sees the snare, and abhors, and runs into it.

People in this state are in bondage to the law and to the spirit of fear. They are described so clearly by the apostle Paul in Romans 7 – those who do the very thing they know is wrong and which they hate. These men and women, Wesley says, are in chains. They are 'under the law'.

But, Wesley continues, there is a third kind of person, one who has been completely liberated from the devil's hold, no longer enslaved to sin, no longer 'under the law'. This person is the one who in Christ enjoys a glorious liberty. As Wesley puts it, this is

> the state of one who has found grace or favour in the sight of God, even the Father, and who has the grace or power of the Holy Ghost, reigning in his heart; who has received, in the language of the Apostle, 'the Spirit of adoption, whereby he now cries, "Abba, Father!"'

See, then, how the enemy will do anything to prevent human beings from leaving their orphan state and becoming the adopted sons and daughters of God. He will do anything to keep men and women in the natural or the legal state because both are forms of slavery. Both are manifestations of the orphan state – the one enslavement to rebellion, the other enslavement to religion. The enemy is determined to do this, and every orphaned angelic spirit under his command is intent on serving this one dark goal: to prevent the natural or the legal person graduating to the filial state. The forces of hell are committed to this. They are therefore marshalled to two wicked objectives: to prevent those who have not been freed from becoming free, and to cause those who have become free to revert to slavery and the orphan state. This is what Satan did with Adam and Eve. This is what he did with Israel. It is what he tries to do with us. And this is not the stuff of Hollywood fantasy. It is fact.

God at war

All this is to say that there is a spiritual dimension to Adam's fall from sonship and to the tragic story of Israel's unfaithfulness as a son. Yes, Israel's seasons of disaster were invariably triggered by disastrous ethical choices – in short, by disobedience to the agreement the people had made with their adopting Father in heaven. But at the same time we must never underestimate the depths and the lengths that the adversary of God was prepared to go to in his vengeful and violent rage against the Father, unleashed upon all who, like Adam, are venerated as 'son', or like Eve revered as 'daughter'.

While the strategy of the adversary may lie more at the level of the implicit in the Old Testament, it is without doubt explicit in the New. As has been said before, the Old Testament is the New concealed; the New Testament is the Old revealed.[2] Therefore in the pages of the New Testament the role and the presence of Satan are ratcheted up considerably. His name is mentioned over 30 times. Indeed, he makes an appearance early on in the Synoptic Gospels, trying to entice Jesus to veer away from his destiny as Son, as he did with Adam and indeed Israel. 'If you are the Son of God . . .' he sneers repeatedly (Matthew 4.1–11; Luke 4.1–13).

This is the adversary's purpose. He is an orphaned angel and his perverted passion is to make orphans, both literally and spiritually. At the physical level, his irrational and brutal plan is to fracture families, turning sons and daughters into orphans, and brides into widows. At the spiritual level, his plan is equally malicious. It is to turn spiritual sons and daughters into orphans and slaves, to turn the noble Bride of Christ into a bowed and beaten widow. Nothing has changed. He has been doing this 'since the beginning'.

This leads to one and only one destination, and that is death. Eve's and Adam's sin has led to death at both the physical and the spiritual level. At the physical level, all of us have an appointment with death, and the fear of death lurks under the surface of every heart because death means separation, and separation is the orphan's nightmare. At the spiritual level, all of us by nature are separated from the Father's love, and the dreadful realization that we are alone in an orphaned cosmos casts a shadow over our souls. At both the physical and the spiritual level, we die. Death is our inheritance.

But the grand story of the Bible shows that our adopting Father was not prepared to leave it at that. The people of Israel might have failed to fulfil God's dream for a son, but there was another. A man was about to appear on the stage of history who would live a life of perfect sonship. He would succeed where Israel had failed.

Born of the line of David, this son would grow up and live as Israel had been called to live.

He would call God '*Abba*, Father', and be known as 'the Son of God'.

He would only do what he saw his Father doing and only say what he heard his Father saying.

He would obey and fulfil the Torah, even going beyond its requirements.

He would embrace his sonship and his kingship, relating intimately to his Father and bringing the rule of God to earth, with signs, miracles and wonders.

He would in every respect, both internally in his heart and externally in his conduct, show us what sonship really looks like.

Israel's failure to live as a son would not be the last word. The triune God was at war. 'No more orphans!' was the cry from heaven.

The orphan-maker was about to meet his match. To use the closing words of the Old Testament, one was about to come who would turn the hearts of orphaned children towards their father – their true Father, who is in heaven.

Hallowed be his name!

6

A mighty deliverance

———•◆•———

When I was a boy, I used to love the Christmas carol service by candlelight at Bradfield College where my adoptive father was a teacher. I remember going many times with my mother and my brother and sister and sitting in the pews, waiting for the service to begin. There was always a hush as the moment approached. The candles would flicker in the college chapel as the choristers took their places in the chancel. Then the opening carol would be sung, usually with a beautifully executed solo, and I would be transported back to 'royal David's city'. It was enchanting.

By far the most impressive moment for me was when my father went to the lectern and read the Prologue from the Gospel of John. There he would stand, his black robe gathered around his shoulders, peering through his black-rimmed spectacles at the Bible. And then he would begin to take us back to creation, in a reading voice that was more resonant than any other that I had ever heard or have ever heard since:

> In the beginning was the Word, and the Word was with God, and the Word was God. He was with God in the beginning. Through him all things were made; without him nothing was made that has been made. In him was life, and that life was the light of all mankind. The light shines in the darkness, and the darkness has not overcome it.　　　(John 1.1–4)

It is hard to describe the impact these words made on me every time I heard them. I am not sure I understood what they really meant. I am not entirely sure that I understand them now. All I know was that my dad was talking about eternal realities, about heavenly light penetrating and conquering our earthly darkness, setting us free.

Today of course I realize that John was allowing us to catch a glimpse of the Incarnation, the history-changing moment when the eternal Son of God was born:

> The true light that gives light to everyone was coming into the world. He was in the world, and though the world was made through him, the world did not recognise him. He came to that which was his own, but his own did not receive him. Yet to all who did receive him, to those who believed in his name, he gave the right to become children of God – children born not of natural descent, nor of human decision or a husband's will, but born of God. (John 1.9–13)

Looking back, it seems to me now that there is something strangely significant about an adopted child listening to his dad reading these words. For John makes it clear that the Word who was made flesh was the only Son of the Father. This Son lived in the closest relationship with the Father in heaven, near to the Father's heart. This Son came to earth to make us the children of God.

Today it never ceases to fill me with wonder that when the Son took oxygen into his tiny human lungs, the world was poised for its deliverance, and orphans were on the very cusp of their adoption.

The fullness of time

In the last chapter we looked at how Israel, like Adam, was called to sonship but fell into slavery. Thankfully, Israel's failure to fulfil its destiny as God's adopted son was tragic but it was not terminal. In Israel a child born in the line of David was to be born. In this Jewish boy, human beings would find their way back into the arms of their Father.

It is the apostle Paul who describes this turning point in Galatians 4.4–7, a passage that more than any other in the New

Testament uncovers the deep purposes behind the life and death of the Father's Son:

> When the set time had fully come, God sent his Son, born of a woman, born under the law, to redeem those under the law, that we might receive adoption to sonship. Because you are his sons, God sent the Spirit of his Son into our hearts, the Spirit who calls out, '*Abba*, Father.' So you are no longer a slave, but God's child; and since you are his child, God has made you also an heir.

Notice what Paul says at the start of this passage: 'When the set time had fully come...' Two millennia ago, there was a moment of unique, divinely orchestrated opportunity. 'Now, Son,' the Father cried in heaven. 'Now is the time to rescue my lost sons and daughters.'

So the Son was 'born of a woman', the Jewish virgin known in her own mother tongue as Miriam. God was the child's Father, but Miriam was his mother. The baby in Bethlehem was accordingly both fully divine and fully human.

This same child was also born 'under the law'. In other words, like every other person in Israel's history, Jesus was born into an environment where God's holy Torah was to be heard and obeyed. He was born with a challenge over his life – a challenge that adopted Israel had failed to meet.

Did Jesus find it any easier than his fellow Jews to obey the Torah? The answer to this has to be 'no'. To save us, he had to be one of us. He was therefore not born 'unable to sin', but born 'able not to sin'. He was born with our flesh.

Jesus did not appear with some perfected version of human flesh, one protected from temptation and immune to sin. No, his flesh was like every other person's flesh. It was not inherently predisposed towards hearing and obeying the law. It had the same inclination towards rebellion as ours. Yet Jesus never sinned. From the womb to the tomb he resisted temptation and lived in total obedience to his Father.

In short, he lived like a son, not an orphan.

Loving God

The apostle Paul states unequivocally that this same Jesus who was born under the law redeemed us from the law.

To comprehend the power of this truth we need to remind ourselves what Jesus himself said about the Torah. He expressed the heart and soul of the Father's instructions to Israel in Mark 12.29–31. When asked by a teacher of the law what the greatest commandment was, Jesus replied:

> The most important one . . . is this: 'Hear, O Israel: the Lord our God, the Lord is one. Love the Lord your God with all your heart and with all your soul and with all your mind and with all your strength.' The second is this: 'Love your neighbour as yourself.' There is no commandment greater than these.

Here we see the heart of the Father. The teachers of Jesus' day had created a love of law – a law-based holiness. Jesus subverts this completely by exposing the real intention behind the Torah, which was to create a law of love. Loving the Father with the totality of one's personhood was the original intention. Loving others as oneself would flow naturally from this filial devotion.

This is what Israel had failed to do. As God's beloved child, chosen from among all the nations, Israel had not loved God with the adoration of a grateful, adopted child. Its people had allowed the Adamic virus to infect their attitude towards the Father. Instead of engaging in a lifestyle of joyful obedience, they had succumbed to an orphan-hearted rebellion against the Love of all loves. Instead of protecting and nurturing a healthy attachment to their adoptive Father, the people of Israel ran after unhealthy attachments, or to use the biblical word, 'idolatry'.

But now, out of Israel, comes a man who through the whole of his life loves the Father with the totality of his being. At every moment, he loves the one whom he calls '*Abba*, Father'. He never wavers from this. His affection for his Father, continually baptized by the fire of the Spirit's love, remains undiminished from start to finish. Even when tempted, this Son by nature does not resort to the orphan-hearted rebellion of the First Adam. This Son holds his course and unswervingly says 'no' to the seductions of the orphan-maker.

This love the Son has for his adoring Father is everything that the Father had wished for in his adopted son, Israel. As such, Jesus fulfils the Father's dreams for Israel. He embodies and exhibits everything that Israel had been destined to become. This is why Jesus' story in many places recapitulates aspects of Israel's story. Why else would Jesus have chosen 12 disciples if it wasn't at least in part because he was called to recapture and complete the mandate given to the 12 tribes of Israel?

Jesus therefore doesn't replace Israel any more than the Church does. He fulfils Israel's calling. He chooses sonship over slavery every time.

So this is why Jesus comes to redeem us from the law. To orphan-hearted Israelites, the law had become a curse, not a blessing. Stripped of its original ethic of love, the law had become a reminder of the standards that seemed forever unattainable. Instead of being the loving instructions of a Father towards a child, God's laws had been turned by the orphan-maker into the oppressive demands of a master towards a slave. The choice that then presented itself was either rebellion or religion, but both turned out in the end to be toxic because both are forms of slavery – the one to rebellious hedonism, the other to religious legalism.

Of course, whichever way a child of Israel turned, he or she ended up under the tyrannical control of the orphan-maker. If individuals chose to indulge in sin, then the enemy of their souls could whip them with the accusation: 'Not good enough'. But if they chose the path of trying to obey countless religious rules and regulations, the adversary could again afflict their conscience with the same accusation: 'Not good enough'. Whether a person chose to be a hedonist or a legalist, the enemy had a hold over him or her. The law, designed to be a blessing, had become a curse, and the curse was, 'You don't measure up.'

It is within this Jewish context that the Son grows up, studying Torah as a Jewish boy, living it with complete fidelity as a Jewish man. Never at any point is he driven by whips of religious legalism. At every moment, rather, he is led by cords of intimate love. In short, he doesn't try to obey Torah out of religious servitude. He hears and obeys the instructions of heaven because he loves his Father with an everlasting love, a love that cannot begin to countenance any kind of breach in his relationship with the one whom he so endearingly and sincerely calls his *Abba*.

For Jesus, then, it is his *delight* to obey his Father's law. This is the way of sonship. It is completely unthinkable for Jesus to begin to contemplate wounding his Father's heart by choosing to engage in orphan behaviour. For Jesus, breaking a law is unimaginable because it would mean breaking a heart – the Father's heart. For one whose entire life and being is dedicated to loving God (in obedience to the *Shema Yisrael*), this is non-negotiable. Jesus fulfils the destiny of Israel, not from some love of law, but out of the law of love. His holiness is accordingly love-based. It is a purity that flows from the wellspring of intimacy.

Loving one's neighbour

If Jesus behaves like a Son in relation to the Father, he also behaves like a brother in relation to his neighbour. In fact, he is the perfect brother.

At this point we should recall one of Jesus' most disturbing parables – about Lazarus, a beggar at the gates of a rich man's luxurious home (Luke 16.19–31). Jesus here tells a short story about a complacent wealthy man who dresses in purple robes and fine linen, dining every day with his five brothers, while outside the gates of his walled estate a poor and sick beggar longs to eat the scraps that fall from the rich man's table.

But then the tables are turned, as it were. The poor man dies and is carried by angels to heaven's banqueting hall. The rich man also dies but he ends up in the fires of hell, desperate for Lazarus to come and bring him just a drop of the water that he is enjoying in the presence of Abraham, the first patriarch of Israel.

Abraham steps in and rebukes the rich man. The die has been cast. The chasm between them is now fixed. No one can cross over from heaven to hell, let alone from hell to heaven.

Realizing that his sentence is not commutable, the rich man exhibits a last vestige of unselfishness. He asks Father Abraham to send Lazarus from heaven to earth, to his five brothers who are living exactly as he had lived. 'Let him warn them,' the rich man pleads, 'so that they will not come to this place of torment.'

But Abraham refuses. 'Even if someone like Lazarus was to rise from the dead and pass on this message, those brothers of yours wouldn't listen.'

There is so much one could draw from this story, but the point I want to emphasize is one that can only be appreciated if you read this parable through Jewish eyes. If you do that, then you will remember the Jewish fondness for number symbolism. You will in particular remember the importance of the number seven, which in Jewish thought denotes 'perfection'.

How many brothers did the rich man have? He had five. How many did that make in total? Including the rich man, it makes six. What would have happened had these six brothers treated Lazarus like a brother rather than a beggar? Then there would have been seven. Seven is the perfect number.

What has this to do with Jesus' obedience to Torah?

There were two parts to Jesus' summary of Torah in Mark chapter 12. The first was the call to love God with the totality of one's being. This, if you will, is the call to adore God as a son adores his father. The second was the call to love one's neighbour as oneself. This, if you will, is the call to love one's neighbour as one loves a brother or sister.

In light of all this, we can see that Jesus is the faithful natural Son who, unlike the adopted son Israel, fulfils the Torah in both its God-focused and human-focused dimensions. He loves God with absolutely everything he has – heart, mind, soul and strength. He also loves his fellow man and woman as he loves himself, visiting others with that same honour, kindness and compassion with which he treats himself.

In this respect the Son practises what he preaches. At the level of human relationships as well as in his relationship with the Father, Jesus models the message. Sinful and destitute people are his sisters and brothers.

So, unlike the rich man in the parable, Jesus' meal tables are full of broken people. Sinners, tax collectors and prostitutes are welcome. The table of Jesus is accordingly an open table. People of all kinds are invited to come as they are. In the presence of the Father's love, however, they are not going to stay as they have been. In the life-transforming atmosphere of these messianic meals, beggars become brothers, and prostitutes become princesses. In that respect, the meals themselves are indeed the message. They are a picture of the kingdom of heaven on earth. They are colourful icons of the culture of heaven where the love of God and the love of one's neighbour are as inexorable as they are inextricable.

Delighting in obedience

Jesus succeeded where Israel failed. As the Son by nature, he heard and obeyed Torah throughout his life. He only said what he heard his *Abba* saying and he only ever did what he saw his *Abba* doing. So precious was his communion with the Father that he never for one moment succumbed to the kind of temptation that would have grieved the Holy Spirit within him and brought his Father to the point of tears. For him, obedience to the Torah was a necessity, but it was a necessity born of relationship, not of religion. Thus, personal holiness – rooted as it was in love, not law – was a delight and not just a discipline. He rejoiced in loving God with all his heart, mind, soul and strength, and in loving his neighbour as himself.

In Psalm 40, King David wrote:

> Sacrifice and offering you did not desire –
>> but my ears you have opened –
>> burnt offerings and sin offerings you did not require.
> Then I said, 'Here I am, I have come –
>> it is written about me in the scroll.
> I desire to do your will, my God;
>> your law is within my heart.'   (verses 6–8)

That is the NIV. The New Living Translation ends with 'I take joy in doing your will, my God, for your instructions are written on my heart.' That is more faithful to the meaning of the word *Torah*.

The author of the Letter to the Hebrews, after discussing the inadequacy of animal sacrifices for dealing with human sin, puts the same words on the lips of God's Son:

Therefore, when Christ came into the world, he said:

> 'Sacrifice and offering you did not desire,
>> but a body you prepared for me;
> with burnt offerings and sin offerings
>> you were not pleased.
> Then I said, "Here I am – it is written about me
>> in the scroll –
> I have come to do your will, my God."'
>> (Hebrews 10.5–7)

What more evidence do we need that Jesus delighted in a love-based obedience to the Father? Every day he found great joy in fulfilling the law. He loved his Father and he loved his neighbour.

In short, he showed us what it truly means to live like a son or a daughter of God.

The end of accusation

And here is where the miracle begins.

By being the first person in human history to live his entire life in obedience to the Torah, Jesus began to reverse the curse that the human race had been under since the fall. This reversal was made possible because Jesus accepted the call to embrace a total identification with our humanity. He was one of us, and in being one of us he took on the same flesh as ours with its inclination to turn back to slavery – only he never sinned. Living as a sinless son of Adam, he started to heal our human nature. In other words, Jesus identified with us so that he could begin to bring our human nature out of the depths of its orphan condition to the heights of heaven where the doors of the Father's house were now open. All this is because Jesus lived and died as a perfect son.

How then did his death affect us?

The apostle Paul answers in Galatians 4.4–7 by saying that Jesus redeemed us from the law. In other words, by living and dying in total obedience to the Torah, Jesus took all the condemnation the law required, and died the death that the law demanded.

This is where we need to remember that the agony of living under the law consisted of constantly recognizing that we didn't measure up to the Father's loving instructions. Every time we failed, the orphan-maker would reinforce the sense of separation from the Father and the consequent shame in our souls by bringing one accusation after another: 'You've failed. You're a loser. You're an orphan.'

Understanding this, the lights should come on in our hearts. We should suddenly recognize, if we haven't already, that God is not our accuser; Satan is. What is it that Satan is called in Revelation 12.10? He is called 'the accuser of [the] brethren' (AV). It is therefore not God who torments his orphaned children. It is Satan. Using the high standards of the Torah, he loves to bring condemnation after condemnation upon our already downcast hearts. 'See how you've failed,' he mocks.

It is precisely here that the Son of God brings deliverance from the oppression of the law. He lives his whole life in total alignment to the Father's will and the Father's ways. He is 100 per cent obedient from the beginning to the end, because he loves his Father relentlessly and loves his orphaned brothers and sisters unceasingly. When the perfect Son dies upon the cross, he dies obedient even unto death. And when he dies, he takes all the accusations and condemnations of Satan and declares them null and void.

See then how wrong it is to propose that the Son takes all the rage and condemnation of his Father at Calvary. The Father is not the accuser. Satan is. On the cross, Jesus destroys any right the enemy has to accuse him. If we choose to live 'in Christ', then this applies to us as well. There is no condemnation or accusation any more. Christ has redeemed us from the law. He has bought us, releasing us from the authority of a demonic and legalistic master, namely Satan. We are no longer driven by the satanic slave-master to live as orphans. We are redeemed by the great chain-breaker to live as sons and daughters.

Thanks to the Son of God, the accuser has been silenced. There is now no charge brought against those who are in Christ Jesus. Our slavery is brought to an end. With the help of the Holy Spirit we can now do what Israel couldn't do, and live as sons and daughters who delight in doing the Father's will.

The defeat of the enemy

There is no better ending for this chapter than Paul's rousing words about the victory of the cross in Colossians 2.13–15. There he writes:

> He forgave us all our sins, having cancelled the charge of our legal indebtedness, which stood against us and condemned us; he has taken it away, nailing it to the cross. And having disarmed the powers and authorities, he made a public spectacle of them, triumphing over them by the cross.

This victorious declaration describes how the Father redeemed us from the law. He did this by achieving two great goals at the cross.

The first goal can be summed up in the word 'cancellation'. Through his death on the cross, Jesus Christ took all the accusations of the enemy – accusations in which the devil incessantly snarled that we didn't measure up – and he cancelled them once and for all. This is because, when the orphan-maker tried to find grounds to accuse the Son of God, no such grounds could be found either in Christ's life or death. As Jesus said, 'The prince of this world is coming but he has nothing on me' (see John 14.30–31). Put another way, 'The accuser is coming but he'll not be able to find any charge against me. I have obeyed and fulfilled Torah in full.'

Thanks to the Son's obedience, then, we no longer have to live with a sense of indebtedness to the law of God and a sense of condemnation over our failures. There has been a permanent cancellation of the debt we owe because of our failure to obey the law. We are accordingly slaves no more.

The Son's love-based sacrifice has silenced the enemy's law-based condemnation. The slave-driver has therefore lost his whip. We no longer need to feel the sting of his constant naming and shaming. We are free!

But there is more.

Not only has there been cancellation; there has also been humiliation. The devil – and his army of powers and principalities – has been conquered. He has been disarmed of his chief weapons, accusation and condemnation, and he has been publicly humiliated as a result of Christ's obedience to death, even death on a cross.

How has he been humiliated?

He has been humiliated because his own perverted tactics actually created the conditions for our liberation. If it hadn't been for Satan motivating Christ's enemies to betray and crucify God's Son, our indebtedness to the law would never have been cancelled and our chains of slavery would never have been broken.

Satan therefore disarmed himself. In helping God to cancel the accusations against us, Satan made himself redundant as the accuser. He did himself out of a job. In that respect he is not only conquered and disarmed; he and his orphaned spirits are made a public laughing stock. His right to shame us was nullified. His days of enslaving spiritual orphans were over.

With the Son's death and resurrection, the chains that bound us broke and fell to the ground.

Prison doors began to open.

Emancipated slaves began to emerge into the daylight, rubbing their eyes.

A mighty deliverance had come.

7

God's daughters and sons

In 1961 my adoptive parents, Philip and Joy Stibbe, entered a London orphanage, took my twin sister and me into their arms, and carried us outside to their car.

Imagine if they had driven halfway home and then stopped beside a desolate wasteland, and turned round and looked at us in our Moses baskets in the back. Imagine if they had said, 'We've got you out of the orphanage, but now we're going to leave you here. We'll keep in touch, though, and send you food parcels.'

Claire and I would have been rescued from the orphanage, and for that we might have learned to become grateful, even sharing that gratitude with others. But we would have never known the real joy of being led out of the orphanage, which was to enter into a new life as a son and a daughter in our father's house.

Missing out on that undeserved life of affection and opportunity, we would have come to see that our rescue was only half a rescue. In time, we would probably have come to question what kind of parent leaves a child free from the hardships of the past but denies that same child any hope for the future. Ultimately, that might well have led us into feeling deeply unsure, not only of the motivation of our parents but also of our own worth.

'Maybe if we'd have been better children, they would have taken us home with them,' we would have sighed.

The whole truth and nothing but

I start with this exaggerated picture because it is not dissimilar to what we have done with the gospel. Too often we have stressed what we have been saved *from*, but failed to explore and experience what we have been saved *to*. This is only half the gospel. It leads people out of the orphanage, but leaves them short of the Father's house.

To make matters worse, the half of the gospel that has been frequently acknowledged has not always been rightly explained. Too often the Western Church has taught that we are saved from the Father's wrath, which Jesus has satisfied and appeased at Calvary. This in turn has led to a profound mistrust of our Father in heaven. For if we are saved from God's wrath at the cross, Jesus saves us in a very real sense from the Father. No wonder then that countless Christians in the West end up loving Jesus but keeping the Father at arm's length. In this we not only divide the Trinity, pitting the Father and the Son against each other, but we also rob people of the assurance that comes from knowing that God is our loving *Abba* Father and we are his eternally adopted sons and daughters.

It is for this and many other reasons that we need to rediscover the truly beautiful story of spiritual adoption that is narrated throughout the pages of the Bible. If we are faithful to this story, then we will be unequivocally clear that our adopting heavenly Father didn't just rescue us from the power of sin and the accuser's condemnations. He also rescued us to enjoy the exhilarating privilege of being his adopted sons and daughters.

This, then, is a more fully orbed picture of salvation.

If we only tell people what they have been rescued from, then the gospel is not really good news at all. It would be like God telling the Hebrew slaves in the desert that they have been rescued from slavery and that alone. That might have given them reassurances about their past, but it would not have granted them a hope for their future.

But this is precisely what the adopting Father does not do. He not only emancipates his people from the whips of Pharaoh's slave-drivers. He also leads them towards a landscape of freedom and abundance, a place flowing with milk and honey, the land where they can truly enjoy unfettered intimacy with God.

In short, he leads them out of slavery into sonship.

As the adopted sons and daughters of such a glorious Father, that is our mandate too. We are to live and preach the whole gospel. On the one hand we are to live free from the shame with which the enemy has taunted us. On the other we are to enter into and enjoy the honour of the Father's delight in calling us daughters and sons.

And we are to help others to receive this matchless honour too.

A balanced gospel

At this point some may be saying, 'That all sounds very well and good, but where is the biblical warrant for such an interpretation of salvation?'

The answer is that it is everywhere. But let us restrict ourselves for the time being to the passage that was the springboard for the previous chapter, Galatians 4.4–5: 'When the set time had fully come, God sent his Son, born of a woman, born under the law, to redeem those under the law, that we might receive adoption to sonship.'

It cannot escape our attention that there are two aspects to what Paul says about our salvation in these verses. He is in no doubt. The death of Jesus brings salvation to an orphaned planet in two ways.

The first of these ways is retrospective. In other words, it points to what we have been rescued *from*. In Paul's mind we have been rescued *from* the law. The death of Jesus Christ has nullified the condemnations and accusations to which we were constantly vulnerable because of our disobedience to the law and our rebellion against God's love.

Those charges are now null and void, and the one who unceasingly reminded us of our moral failures has been stripped of his whip and disarmed of his chief weapon, which was to render us guilty and ashamed. Satan is now off our backs.

But there's more.

Not only are we liberated from the chains of slavery. We are also liberated into a life of sonship. This is the purpose of our salvation. We have been redeemed from the law *so that* we can enjoy the status of sons and daughters.

This for Paul is the gospel. The retrospective blessings of the atonement have to do with being saved from endless condemnation. The prospective blessings of the atonement have to do with being saved to eternal sonship.

The diagram shows what Paul the apostle means by our adoption in Christ.

If this is true, then we cannot just stress the retrospective blessings of the atonement without delighting in its prospective blessings. That would be like remembering Egypt but forgetting the promised land. Nor can we stress the prospective blessings without remembering the retrospective ones. That would be like enjoying the land of milk and honey but forgetting the oppression from which we have been delivered. Both need to be given equal emphasis; otherwise we will believe and proclaim an incomplete gospel. We will leave people halfway between the orphanage from which they have been delivered and the Father's house where they are meant to live, laugh and love.

That, I would suggest, is not true freedom.

The importance of identity

The reason why half the gospel is not true freedom is because a failure to understand and explain the prospective blessings of sonship has two consequences: it causes many believers to misunderstand who God really is, and in the process to misunderstand who they truly are in Christ.

This is in effect an issue of identity – the identity of God (who God truly is, as revealed by his Son) and our identity (who we really are in Christ). Let me show you what the Bible reveals when it comes to these twin issues of divine and human identity.

In my view, the single most important statement of God's plan of salvation is summed up in Paul's breathtakingly beautiful words in 2 Corinthians 6.18: 'I will be a Father to you, and you will be my sons and daughters, says the Lord Almighty.'

Notice the two parts of this statement. Both have to do with identity.

In the first part, the issue is *God's* identity. He wants to be known and worshipped as *Abba* Father. 'I will be a Father to you' is a statement about who he really is in himself and what he really longs to be to us. His dream since the tragedy of Eden has been that spiritual orphans should know him once again as *Abba*. Just as the Son knew God as *Abba*, so the adopted sons and daughters of God are to know him as *Abba* Father too.

This is God's true identity.

But this is not where it ends. The second part of the verse refers to *our* identity. If we are in Christ, we are not to see ourselves as spiritual orphans any more. We are not to cower under the slave-master's whip, living a life of religious servitude. We are to know our new true identity in Christ. Filled with the Spirit of adoption, we are to see ourselves as sons and daughters of the Most High God.

Put in the language of Galatians 4.4–7, we are no longer slaves. We are daughters and sons.

Daughters of the King

Some of you, I am sure, will have rejoiced at the reference to 'daughters' in that last sentence. Perhaps this is the right moment to pause and emphasize the supremely important point that the word 'sonship' doesn't just refer to men who believe in Christ. It refers of course to women as well.

So far in this book the language that I've been using has been undeniably masculine in nature. I have spoken of 'the Father', of Jesus as 'the Son' (and indeed our 'Brother') and Israel as God's adopted 'son'.

Does this mean that the privilege of adoption is given only to male members of the family of God? If so, then in what sense is God truly a loving Father? What kind of father gives gifts to his sons while neglecting his daughters?

The good news is that Jesus died not only to make men sons of God. He died to make women daughters of the King as well. Perhaps nowhere is this more vividly seen than in the second half of the verse just quoted, 2 Corinthians 6.18. Here God says, 'you will be my sons and daughters'.

We will not see how significant the addition of 'daughters' is here unless we recognize the Old Testament Scripture that Paul is quoting. He is referring to 2 Samuel 7.14. This occurs within a passage about David's longing to build the Temple.

Nathan the prophet has a dream in which God asks him to tell David that he is not the one to build God's house. His son Solomon will do that instead. God promises therefore that David's dream will be realized. More than that, he says of David, 'I will be his father, and he shall be my son.' This is the verse that Paul cites in 2 Corinthians 6.18. He applies a promise given about Solomon to every person who receives God's offer of salvation in Christ: 'I will be a Father to you, and you will be my sons and daughters.'

Paul, under the illumination of the Holy Spirit – who is the Spirit of adoption – takes a promise that was originally intended for Solomon and declares that it is fulfilled in the lives of those who receive salvation in Christ. In other words, he pluralizes a statement that was originally singular. 'Son' becomes 'sons' here. That is bold.

What is even bolder is the addition, 'and daughters'. There was no reference to a daughter in the original Old Testament text. But Paul, led by the Holy Spirit – the Spirit who at Pentecost breaks down the dividing walls between men and women – includes daughters too. The apostle who is often accused of being anti-women is insistent here in his inclusiveness: the Father's plan was all along for men to enjoy the identity of sons and for women to enjoy the identity of daughters.

This Father loves his daughters as much as his sons. There is no pro-male bias in the heart of God.

Abba's *inclusive heart*

Even having said that, I am sure that there will still be some for whom the overtly masculine language of sonship is problematic. It is here that it is worth remembering that there are in fact two grand metaphors in the Bible for our new and privileged status in Christ.

The first is filial and has to do with sonship – with us becoming sons by adoption. This is a metaphor that may be easier for men to access.

The second grand metaphor is nuptial. This has to do with the people of God becoming the Bride of Christ – a metaphor that is perhaps easier for women to access.[1]

In the filial metaphor, female disciples have to overcome the hurdle of masculine language. In the nuptial metaphor, male disciples have to overcome the hurdle of feminine language.

The Bible therefore provides two doors into understanding and enjoying intimate communion with the triune God. This reflects the inclusive nature of the Father's heart. No one is to miss out on the opportunity of a personal, heartfelt relationship with God. He is the Father who loves us more than any earthly father ever could. And he is the Bridegroom who adores us more than any earthly husband ever could. If our gender and our experiences make one door difficult, then the other is open to us to try. That is why God offers himself as both Father and Bridegroom. It is now up to us to respond to the overtures of his divine love.

Why does the Bible portray God in such terms? The answer is not just because the Father wants people of both genders to enter into his loving embrace. It is also because his heart beats and bleeds more than anything else for those who have no father and those who have lost their spouse. Throughout the Bible God is known as a Father to the fatherless and a defender of the cause of the widow.

To the orphan he has provided a metaphor that opens up the abandoned heart to the love of the Father. This is the idea of sonship.

To the widow he has provided a metaphor that opens up the grieving heart to the love of the Bridegroom. This is the call to be the Bride of Christ.

We therefore have a Father who wants women as well as men to revel in the knowledge of who he really is, and who they truly are too. He wants us to know him as Father, and he longs for us to see ourselves as his royally adopted and honoured daughters and sons.

Under open heavens

This brings us back to our salvation. Having been saved from a lifestyle of slave-driven performance, we are now released into the undeserved position of being the daughters and sons of God. This is the journey of salvation.

If we are to enter into the fullness of this sonship (in the inclusive sense of the word), we need to learn a whole new way of relating to God – one based not on performance (slavery) but on position (sonship).

For this to happen we have to be conformed to the image of God's Son, Jesus Christ. This is the end-game of both discipleship and sonship. As adopted daughters and sons, we are to become more and more like the Son by nature. Over time, we are to renounce every trace of the orphan virus from our hearts and every hint of slavery from our behaviour, and start to live *from* approval, not *for* approval.

This was the starting point for the whole of Jesus' ministry and mission. Far from trying to earn the Father's approval and affection, Jesus already knew that the Father approved of him and loved him before he said or did anything. He therefore never preached a message or performed a miracle in order to be loved by the Father. He did these things *because* he was already loved.

For Jesus, then, it wasn't a case of *I do; therefore I am*. It was a case of *I am; therefore I do*.

I am loved; therefore I will share the good news of the kingdom. I will minister healing to the sick. I will set the captives free. I will welcome the outcast. I will raise the dead – all because the Father loves me so.

This is evident at Jesus' baptism in the River Jordan. In the account in Mark's Gospel we read:

> At that time Jesus came from Nazareth in Galilee and was baptised by John in the Jordan. Just as Jesus was coming up out of the water, he saw heaven being torn open and the Spirit descending on him like a dove. And a voice came from heaven: 'You are my Son, whom I love; with you I am well pleased.' (Mark 1.9–11)

This is one of those moments in the Gospels when we glimpse the eternal flow of love within the three persons of the holy and undivided family of the Trinity. The Son stands in the river. The Spirit descends upon him. The Father speaks words of timeless affirmation and heavenly affection.

As all this happens, the human heart of the Son of God is overwhelmed by the Father's love. The Holy Spirit, the bond of love between the Father and the Son, and the Son and the Father, brings a fresh and foundational revelation of the Father's unbridled affection into Jesus' human heart – an affection based on who he is, not on what he does.

Standing under an open heaven, the Son is visited by a fatherly approval and affection before he has begun his ministry of proclaiming and demonstrating that the kingdom of heaven has arrived in human history. He is declared to be God's Son before he says or does anything publicly.

And this is not an adoption into sonship. It is an affirmation of an already existing sonship. Jesus is the Son of God before he enters our space and time as a human being. He is the Son of God after he leaves and ascends to the Father in heaven. He is forever the only Son by nature.

When he stands in the river, he is not made something that he was not before. He is affirmed for who and what he already is: the one and only Son of the Father.

Come to the river

So this is the starting point for the person who is to live as a daughter or a son by adoption. Like Jesus, we are to live out of love, not fear. We are not to be timid and unsure of God's love for us, seeking always to earn his pleasure through the things that we say and do for him. That is what it means to live under the law. It is a life fraught with the fear of disapproval and punishment. Rather, we are to know in the deepest recesses of our spirits that we are the children of God and that the Father himself loves us dearly, not because of what we say and do, but because in Christ we stand beneath an open heaven and hear these words spoken over us: 'You are my beloved child! My chosen one! My delight!'

When we live under such open heavens, we are truly daughters and sons by adoption. For us, perfect love – the Father's love – has driven out all fear of divine disapproval and punishment. We can now live with the realization that the Father has lavished his love upon us and freely given us the extraordinary honour of being called children of God (1 John 3.1). This revelation then completely subverts and inverts the default setting for living a fruitful life. Instead of living *for* approval, we now start living *from* approval. Instead of gaining a sense of worth from what we do, we derive our worth from who we are.

In this way we never languish in the dreadful feeling that we don't measure up. To be sure, we mess up, fall and fail. But we no longer let the devil whip us, nor do we beat ourselves up. We stand up tall, enter the river again and thank the Father that his adoptive love is unconditional, not conditional; it is eternal, not ephemeral.

This then is the starting point for the adopted son or daughter. Daily we need to enter the river, see the heavens open and hear the words of our loving, heavenly *Abba* – words that remind us who he really is and also who we are.

Basking in Abba's *love*

How then does this revelation of the fatherly love of God come to us?

It comes to us the same way as it did with the Son by nature. Jesus received the affirmation and affection of the Father through the Holy Spirit who descended on him like a dove at his baptism. This same Spirit of God also works in those who are sons and daughters by adoption. The Holy Spirit is the fire of divine love that ignites the believer's heart with a holy affection for God. Without that same bond of the Spirit which flows between the Son by nature and his Father, we would still feel like spiritual orphans. But with the help of the Spirit, we are gathered up into the Son's relationship with the Father, and in the process we learn to address God with the same adoring *Abba* cry that the ascended Jesus eternally utters. When that happens, we begin to experience the priceless gift of assurance that we have communion with the triune God.

In Galatians 4.6–7, Paul teaches his readers how the Holy Spirit makes all the difference in this matter of knowing the Father's love as sons and daughters by adoption. For him, the gift of sonship has been secured as a result of the finished work of the cross. The death of Jesus has rescued us from slavery and placed us in God's eternal family as sons and daughters by adoption. That is an objective fact. But the key to making it a subjective reality is the Holy Spirit. As Paul declares:

> Because you are his sons, God sent the Spirit of his Son into our hearts, the Spirit who calls out, '*Abba*, Father.' So you are no longer a slave, but God's child; and since you are his child, God has made you also an heir. (Galatians 4.6–7)

Paul has just spoken about the retrospective and prospective blessings of salvation. Thanks to the death of Jesus we have been redeemed from the law and adopted into sonship. How then is a person to know the reality of this adoptive life of God? The answer is in the very next statement. God sends the same Holy Spirit, who abides forever in the Son by nature, into the hearts of those who are sons and daughters by adoption. Notice the word 'hearts' here. This is no cerebral matter. This is an affective reality. Out of inflamed, love-filled hearts the adopted son or daughter of God now cries, '*Abba*, Father', when addressing God. The newborn child of God addresses the King of the universe as 'Papa', 'dearest Father', or 'Daddy'.

Only through the agency of this Spirit of love is such a heartfelt cry possible. When a person becomes an adopted child of God, he or she enters into the reality of what it means to know God as *Abba* through receiving the Holy Spirit. To be sure, faith is required too. For Paul, believing that Jesus is the Son of God by nature is a prerequisite. But receiving the Holy Spirit of adoption is vital too. Believing and receiving need to go together. How and when exactly these two interact is a matter of great debate. For me, the important issue has never been exactly when and how these things happen, because trying to contain the work of the Spirit in a tidy theological statement is as difficult as tying down a tornado. The important thing is simply to believe the gospel and receive the Spirit, and to experience our own exodus from slavery to sonship.

Receiving the Spirit of adoption is therefore essential. The primary ministry of the Holy Spirit is the ministry of adoption. This means that our theology of the Holy Spirit, if we have one, cannot bypass the relational dynamics of the Spirit's work. Perhaps in this respect there should be some realignment in the way we sometimes speak about the Spirit of God. Too often the emphasis is more upon power than love. Yet the Spirit of God is the bond of love that unites the Father with the Son, and the Son with the Father. The Spirit of God is also the bond of love that elevates us into the ascended life of the Son, where we are seated in the heavenly realms in constant awe of the Father's amazing love.

The Spirit of God is therefore the fire of God's love that sets our hearts ablaze with the knowledge of God's extravagant grace, evidenced in the fact that we are adopted as his sons and daughters and are therefore the royally privileged and undeserving children of the living God.

We cannot underestimate the importance of the loving work of the Spirit of adoption. If Jesus needed the Holy Spirit and the affirmation of the Father, then we do too.

Venerating Jesus' life

From all of this we should start to see, if we don't already, that it is not just Jesus' death that has saving significance for us. His life does too. If Jesus' death is the means by which we are led out of slavery and into sonship, Jesus' life offers us a vision of what that sonship really looks like. The story of Jesus' life shows how we can live as adopted sons and daughters of God in our human flesh.

The entire life of Christ is therefore the life of perfect sonship. If the death of Jesus emancipates us from slavery and empowers us to live as sons and daughters, then the life that he lived as a human being is critical for our salvation because that life is a life of sonship in the flesh – the flesh that inclines to the orphan state. It is the summit and pinnacle of what a human being filled with the Spirit of adoption can become in Christ. Christ shows us in his earthly, incarnate, human life the goal and purpose of salvation, which is to live in the glorious freedom of the sons and daughters of God.

At the same time, Jesus' life of sonship is so much more than merely an example or an inspiration to us. It is something in which we can share. Keep in mind that, according to the apostle Paul, Jesus Christ lived and died, was raised and ascended, as the Last Adam. Just as the First Adam infected the human race with a virus that has led us to be spiritual orphans, so the Last Adam has injected the human race with an antidote that leads us to become spiritual sons and daughters by adoption. The First Adam created slaves. The Last Adam creates sons and daughters.

This means that Jesus' sonship is not just paradigmatic. It is also a sonship in which we can *participate* mystically and personally, through the Spirit of adoption. With the help of the Holy Spirit, we can die to the orphan state, rise into our new status as sons and daughters, ascend into heaven and sit with the Son of God in the heavenly realms, far above all the defeated demonic powers of the universe.

United with Christ, we therefore become new creations. We may still have to live with the proclivities of the First Adam's flesh, but we are now filled with the Last Adam's life.

Looking to the East

When Paul starts his Letter to the Ephesians, he cannot help thanking God for all his blessings:

> Praise be to the God and Father of our Lord Jesus Christ, who has blessed us in the heavenly realms with every spiritual blessing in Christ. For he chose us in him before the creation of the world to be holy and blameless in his sight. In love he predestined us for adoption to sonship through

Jesus Christ, in accordance with his pleasure and will – to the praise of his glorious grace, which he has freely given us in the One he loves.   (Ephesians 1.3–6)

Few passages show more clearly than this that God's purpose from before all time was that estranged and exiled human beings should receive adoption as daughters and sons. Before the world was created, the God and Father of our Lord Jesus Christ already had a rescue plan. He knew in advance that the orphan-maker would tempt his beloved son and daughter in the garden, turning them from sonship to slavery, from heirs into orphans. So he planned ahead of time that his Son would die at Calvary so that human beings could be redeemed from slavery and adopted as his sons and daughters. It is this proactive, adopting love that causes Paul's heart to swell with praise.

Our destiny is therefore much greater than the vision of life so often provided by religion. The revelation of the big story of Scripture contains a far greater dream – the Father's dream for us. His dream is that one day we would accept the invitation to come and stand in the river with Jesus, and that in Christ we should hear the Father's voice and receive the Spirit's touch. His vision, in short, was that we should enjoy intimate communion with the triune God.

In entering such a communion, the plan was that we should exercise our authority as God's daughters and sons to bring heaven to those who are experiencing hell on earth. In other words, it was to restore the original mandate given to Adam and Eve, a mandate of sonship and kingship, a mandate to relate and to rule. This is what Jesus, the Last Adam, does. He lives in communion with the Father as the Son of God and he declares that the kingdom of heaven is at hand, confirming this with signs and wonders. This is what we are called to do as well – to pray, 'Our Father in heaven' and 'Your kingdom come'.

In light of this, any doctrine of salvation that omits 'adoption into sonship' is incomplete. As I wrote at the start of this chapter, it leads people out of the orphanage but leaves them short of the Father's house. God's purpose was that we should be brought home from the far country of rebellion and return to our heart's true home in his arms of love. It was his longing from the beginning that we should be orphans no more, but rather led like Israel out of slavery into sonship. This is why Jesus lived and died in the way he did – so that we could enjoy communion with the triune God.

It is here that those of us who have been brought up in the Western Catholic or Protestant traditions need to listen with humble hearts and open ears to those in the Eastern Orthodox tradition. As Kharalambos Anstall has very clearly articulated, in the Orthodox tradition the reason why Christ came to earth was to bring about 'the union of fallen man with the Holy Trinity'. The purpose of the atonement is therefore not, in Anstall's view, about penal substitution, for 'what sort of love would require a supposedly adoring father to demand the agony, torment, and bloody sacrifice of his only son to accomplish the fulfillment of his own selfish satisfaction?'[2] To Anstall at least, this is 'theological nonsense' and even 'blasphemy'.[3]

No, the purpose of the atonement in Eastern Orthodoxy is 'loving communion with God' through 'a recapitulation of human nature'.[4] It is, in other words, a relational, not a legal or 'juridical', purpose.

God's plan was that 'we may forever enjoy a filial relationship (in adopted sonship) with the Father'[5] – 'a relationship of intense intimacy of personal and reciprocal love'.[6]

Maybe it's time for those of us in the West to look to the East.

8

Why have you abandoned me?

What is it like to be an orphan?

I'll tell you.

To grow up as an orphan is to grow up with a primal wound at the very core of your being.

My twin sister and I were separated from our birth mother shortly after we were born. Our mother had been a young woman in her late teens and had decided to give us up for adoption. Our biological father had left the scene, not even knowing of our existence. We were therefore introduced to the world without a father and with the stigma of being illegitimate, something about which we were from time to time reminded in our childhood and teens. Occasionally the word 'bastard' was used to drive the point home.

If you have ever been abandoned like this, you will know what it is to grow up with an orphan heart. The orphan-heart condition is something I've written about extensively, so there is no need to labour the point here. It is sufficient to say that there are two constants when it comes to this wound. The first is *separation* (from the love of your biological parents) and the second is *shame* (a fundamental sense of being defective and flawed).

How do these play out?

In the first instance, the orphan feels the acute pain of separation from a father's love and a mother's love too. This *act* of separation creates, in turn, *feelings* of separation. These feelings morph into one of two things.

The first is a sense of *rejection*. Rejection is the agonizing feeling that you have been wilfully discarded or thrown away.

'Rejection' is a cruel word with connotations of being treated like garbage. To reject another human being is brutal. The statement 'You're a reject' is one of the most abusive that can be hurled at a person.

The second is a sense of *abandonment*. This appears less severe, because when parents abandon their child, they very often don't intend or want to hurt the one they are abandoning. They may even think they are doing him or her a favour. Nevertheless, the child being abandoned ends up feeling left behind and alone.

Whether a person feels deliberately rejected or reluctantly abandoned, the wound is excruciating. When such separation occurs, it doesn't matter to the orphan whether the motivations of the parent were good or not. The orphan *feels* rejected or abandoned, even if he or she comes to *think* that there were legitimate grounds for the separation. Emotion always trumps reason.

These feelings then play into the second aspect of the orphan-heart condition, which is shame. Shame, as has been pointed out many times, is not the same as guilt. Shame is a *being* word. Guilt is a *doing* word. Shame is ontological while guilt is functional. The first targets our sense of who we are, the second what we've done.

When children are rejected or abandoned, toxic shame begins to grip their heart. If they were rejected, they end up feeling like they were, and indeed are, rubbish. If they were abandoned, they end up feeling as if that separation would never have happened had they been a better, more lovable person.

The world in which we live today is in the grip of a global pandemic of fatherlessness. Countless numbers of children on every continent are experiencing separation from a father's love (and sometimes a mother's too) and are consequently living without honour and with a debilitating and gnawing sense of shame. Separated from their fathers, they are disconnected from the person who would have told them, 'You're my son, my daughter, and I'm proud of you.' This in turn leads to a crushing sense in a child's fragile heart that he or she is a mistake, an accident, a failure, a loser.

The world is full of orphans – people like my sister and me, who know separation and shame.

The human condition

What is true at this sociological level is also true at a spiritual level. In other words, what applies to literal, physical orphans is true for spiritual orphans. The Bible teaches that we are all by nature spiritual orphans. From the Garden of Eden onwards, the legacy of Eve's and Adam's rebellion against the Father's love has been an acute sense of separation from God and a deep-rooted shame. Whether or not the guilt for our first parents' sin is transmitted down the generations is a point that will continue to be hotly debated. But what I think cannot be denied is that we all grow up with a sense that we are not naturally connected to the Father's love and so we feel ashamed. This drives us into desperately trying to earn a sense of value and honour through counterfeits or substitutes of God's approval and affection. Driven by the need to feel valued, people stop at nothing to be successful and wealthy, hoping that their achievements will somehow remove or at least anaesthetize the primal pain within.

The orphan-heart condition is a consequence of the fall. When we look back through the gates of Eden, we can see how both separation and shame take root in our first parents' hearts.

First of all, Adam and Eve experience separation. Having enjoyed intimacy with the Father, walking and talking with the triune God in the blossoming garden, they now experience separation. Having sinned, they cannot face being in their *Abba's* presence. So they hide, preferring a world of shadowy absence to the brilliant light of his smile.

Then the man and his wife heard the sound of the LORD God as he was walking in the garden in the cool of the day, and they hid from the LORD God among the trees of the garden. But the LORD God called to the man, 'Where are you?'

He answered, 'I heard you in the garden, and I was afraid because I was naked; so I hid.' (Genesis 3.8–10)

Second, Adam and Eve experience a sense of shame. Realizing that they have rebelled against their Father's love, they suddenly see themselves as naked. They see themselves as defective and this causes them to be afraid. Fear then makes them try to control their situation, frantically sewing leaves together to provide a makeshift covering for their shame.

Then the blame game begins. Adam tells God it was Eve's fault. Eve tells God it was the serpent's fault.

And the rest is history. We have been separated and ashamed ever since.

Cometh the hour, cometh the Man!

But then a man arrives on the stage of history to rescue fallen humanity from its orphan state.

His name is Jesus.

He is the Father's one and only Son by nature (John 3.16).

He has come to earth from eternity, where he has dwelt close to the Father's heart (John 1.18).

He alone reveals the Father's character and tells the Father's story, saying, 'No one knows the Son except the Father, and no one knows the Father except the Son and those to whom the Son chooses to reveal him' (Matthew 11.27).

This man lives a life of perfect sonship, showing all the spiritual orphans what they can now become if they accept his offer of rescue (John 1.12–13).

They can come running home into the Father's loving arms (Luke 15.20).

They can become the adopted sons and daughters of a Father who will never reject or abandon them, never leave nor forsake them (John 6.37; Hebrews 13.5).

They can learn to address the God of the universe as 'our Father', just as Jesus does (Matthew 6.9).

They can then experience an end to the Adamic separation from the Father's love and the shame that has blighted the human condition since Eden (Romans 5.17).

They can enjoy intimate communion with the triune God and the superlative honour of hearing the Father rejoicing over them with singing, and declaring both in heaven and on earth, 'You are my beloved child' (Matthew 3.17).

They can learn to proclaim with the apostle John, 'See what great love the Father has lavished on us, that we should be called children of God! And that is what we are!' (1 John 3.1).

They can live as sons and daughters, not as orphans and slaves, enjoying the status of co-heirs with the Son of God (Galatians 4.7).

They can take the Father's love to the fatherless (John 4.23; James 1.27).

They can become the source of hope and healing to an orphaned planet (Romans 8.19).

The miraculous exchange

How, then, did this possibility become a reality for our orphaned planet?

The answer is: because something seismic occurred in and through the coming of the Son of God. As a result of his birth, life, death, resurrection and Ascension, something has changed dramatically in our orphan state. A great and marvellous transformation has taken place – a cosmic exodus from slavery to sonship.

Jesus, the perfect Son of God, has taken on our human flesh, with all its inherited inclinations towards separation from the Father's love and toxic shame.

He has lived a life in constant and intimate communion with his heavenly Father, living under the honour of the Father's affirmation, 'This is my beloved Son.'

He has obeyed the Torah, the Father's instructions, in full, living as a son should live before his Father, doing what we could not do for ourselves.

He has disarmed the slave-driver Satan at the cross, declaring his condemnations and accusations of us null and void by absorbing them in his tortured body.

He has suffered the anger of every orphan at Calvary, soaking up our rebellion and rage, choosing to pray, 'Father, forgive them, for they know not what they do.'

He has been buried in the ground but raised from the dead, and in his bodily resurrection has been vindicated and confirmed as the Father's one and only Son by nature.

In rising from the dead, he has transformed the way human beings can relate to God, turning slaves into friends, and orphans into sons and daughters.

In ascending and returning home to the Father, he has blazed a trail to the Father's house, bringing many sons and daughters into the glory of the Father's embrace.

Seated at the right hand of the majesty on high, he has poured out his Father's priceless gift of the Holy Spirit, the fire of divine love, the Spirit of adoption.

A mighty exodus has therefore happened. Jesus has turned the tables on the enemy. He has broken the chains of our slavery. He has made it possible for us to turn around and come home to the Father.

A history-making promise

In achieving this wonderful transformation, Jesus' death on the cross was pivotal. If the crucified Son had not taken the full impact of the enemy's condemnation – a condemnation we deserved but Christ did not – we would still be slaves, forever trying to measure up to the Father's standards, but never succeeding. This is another way of saying that we would forever have been like spiritual orphans before God, trying to earn his pleasure and approval through our performance, never able to rest simply in our position as sons and daughters. But at the cross, the Son of God changed everything. He died in our place, as our substitute. Having lived the life we couldn't live, he died the death that we deserved. This death was not a matter of the Father inflicting wrath upon his Son but rather, the Son absorbing the rage of our orphaned planet. It was a case of receiving, not the Father's condemnation, but that of the orphan-maker, who has been a legalist since his fall from heaven. Our perfect older Brother died for us so that our separation from the Father's love could be brought to an end and we could experience an ecstatic reconciliation with the Love of all loves in the Father's house. He died in our place so that we might no longer experience the shame of the orphan state but instead know the honour of being the royally adopted sons and daughters of the high King of heaven.

Truly this is a miraculous exchange.

This is why the cross of Christ is so pivotal. Without the cross there would have been no atonement, no at-one-ment, between the lost and orphaned children of this earth and our Father in heaven. There would have been no end to the slavery of the law and no let-up from the accusations of the enemy. We would have been perpetually in Egypt, whipped by the orphan-maker's condemnations, afflicted by shame and haunted by a sense of the absence of God. As such, in relation to God, we would forever have been slaves rather than friends. We would have been perpetually lost in the orphan state.

But the Son of God came into this world and revealed the Father, appealing to every spiritual orphan to see the Father heart of God in his own words and deeds: 'If you've seen me, you've seen the Father' (see John 14.9). And on the night before he died, he looked around at the band of confused disciples at the Passover meal table and decreed, 'I will not leave you as orphans' (John 14.18). What a promise that is!

The disciples had been *orphanoi* (orphans), not *tekna tou theou* (children of God, John 1.12). They had been *douloi* (slaves), not *philoi* (friends, John 15.15). But as Jesus prepares for his death, he says, 'The Father himself loves you dearly' (John 16.27 NLT), and he promises the disciples they are not going to be left as orphans, separated from the Father's love. He's going to come back, and when he does they will be like him, sons and daughters who know the Father.

The torment of separation

What did it cost Jesus to rescue us from our orphan state?

It cost him dear.

Here it is not enough to focus on his physical sufferings, dwelling on the brutality of the Roman soldiers who beat and then crucified him. Those are indeed agonizing, though they are referred to only in passing in the Gospels, with a narrative restraint that has not always characterized the film-maker or the preacher. No, we must also focus on the spiritual pain that Jesus experienced.

When some have attended to the spiritual dimension of Christ's Passion, they have suggested that the Son was the undeserving victim of the Father's rage at Calvary. I have already argued that this is hard to sustain from Scripture, hard to understand theologically and hard to explain today to those who do not believe in God. So I am not convinced that this was the source of Christ's spiritual agony.

My view is that the source of Christ's torment at Calvary was not the Father's anger but the Father's absence – or, more properly speaking, a sense *in the Son's fully human heart* that he had become separated from his Father's love.

Think about it: he who had never once failed to love the Father with all his being, and his neighbour as himself, became sin for our sakes at the cross. One thing that every human being knows about sin, about wilfully rebelling against the Father's love, is that it takes us away from the Father's house into the wastelands of the far country.

If sin takes us away from the light of the Father's presence, then there had to have been some consciousness *in Christ's fully human heart* of an excruciating sense of absence. This absence, this sense of separation from the Father's love, was the price that Jesus had to pay so that we could be rescued from our orphan state. He had to experience the hell of not knowing the Father's presence in order that we should be rescued from the same nightmare of isolation and desolation. He had to go where we go, feel what we feel, experience what we experience; otherwise he would never have been able to draw us out of our abysmal pit of separation and lead us into the bright and warm security of the Father's house.

Jesus therefore went to hell and back for us. He endured the full agony of the orphan plight – living in the shadow of the Father's absence – so that he could bring us into the presence of the Father of lights.

When Jesus promised his disciples, 'I will not leave you as orphans', he therefore knew full well what this was going to cost him personally. It was going to mean that he had to enter into the very fullness of the orphan state. He was going to have to experience what it was like *in his human flesh* to feel separated from *Abba* Father's love.

I stress, 'in his human flesh'. Jesus of Nazareth was fully human as well as fully divine. So what I am suggesting here is not a fracture in the triune God. The Father and the Son were not divided at Calvary, nor was their eternal relationship of love cruelly broken. Rather, *in Jesus' fully human heart* he experienced what it was like to be a spiritual orphan, separated from his *Abba's* love.

How different this is from the start of Jesus' ministry. At his baptism, Mark reports that the heavens were torn open and that the Father spoke words of endearing affirmation and heartfelt affection over his Son. That was without doubt a defining moment for Jesus of Nazareth. To use the beautiful words of Brennan

Manning, Jesus' human heart was 'seized by the power of a great affection'.[1]

When Mark uses the word 'torn' to describe the open heavens, he deliberately sets up a link with the cross, where the veil of the Temple is torn (the same word in the Greek) from top to bottom after Jesus dies. The beginning and the end of Jesus' ministry are accordingly connected in Mark's mind.

If we now link Jesus' baptism in the river with his suffering at the cross, we begin to glimpse something of the vast difference between these two events. For now, at Calvary, the heavens are not open. They feel like brass.

The Father's loving voice is no longer heard. There is silence.

What a contrast we see here.

In order to rescue us from our orphan state, Jesus willingly allowed himself to experience the full agony of what it is like to be separated from the Father's love. This did not mean that he was *actually* separated from his Father within the divine family of the Trinity. It means that he *felt* separated within his human heart and soul.

The cry of the abandoned child

It is hard for anyone who has never experienced what it is like to be orphaned to understand the difference between what was going on in Jesus' heart (the trauma of abandonment) and what he knew in his head ('I am not alone, for my Father is with me', John 16.32).

If, however, you have experienced the primal wound of separation from a father's and mother's love, you will understand very clearly how these two apparently opposing responses can co-exist within the landscape of the same person's experience.

For the orphaned child, *thinking* and *feeling* are not the same. You may come to realize in your head that there was a reason (even a good reason) why your biological parents couldn't keep you, but this doesn't stop you feeling bereft.

Thinking and feeling, therefore, create two different responses within the same soul. Speaking for myself, I have lived for much of my life with a feeling of having been abandoned, as well as a realization that my mother loved me but didn't have the resources to keep my sister and me.

Although this is by no means a perfect analogy, I believe that something not dissimilar was going on in the dying embers of the Son's consciousness at Calvary. Of course we are in the realm of speculation here, for who can really know what is going on in another person's life? Yet it is nevertheless possible to draw a vital distinction.

On the one hand the Son of God knew his relationship with the Father and the Holy Spirit was eternal and unbreakable within the family of the Trinity. On the other hand he also felt this crushing sense that he had been abandoned by his heavenly Father – that he was now in the far country and no longer in the Father's house.

Thinking and feeling may have therefore been two different responses: the first born of *logos* (reason), the second of *pathos* (suffering). As Jesus senses this *feeling* of separation within his human heart, he experiences the primal wound of the orphan, which is separation from a parent's love.

As he experiences this primal wound, he utters the orphan's primal scream.

'Dad, where are you?'

'Mum, where have you gone?'

Or, to use the words that Jesus himself utters, taken from the beginning of Psalm 22 (NLT): 'My God, my God, why have you abandoned me?'

However else we may want to interpret this cry, we cannot avoid the note of intense torment here. Jesus feels that his Father is now far away, not near. He is absent, not present. He is separated, not united.

In his human heart, Jesus *feels* abandoned. He suffers the primal wound of the orphan.

The agony of shame

And this is not all.

In the orphan heart, separation isn't the only source of pain. Shame hurts as well. Shame attaches itself like a parasite to the wound of separation. The orphan-maker uses separation from our parent or parents to accuse us of being somehow defective, a sham, a mistake. In the face of such mocking taunts, the orphan heart goes from one depth of worthlessness to another.

While some may want to argue the point when it comes to Jesus feeling separated from the Father at Calvary, no one can contest the fact that Jesus experienced the most intense kind of shame imaginable. Crucifixion was the slave's death (*servile supplicium*, as Cicero called it). It left the person totally without honour and dignity, naked and exposed to scornful eyes and the unmerciful elements.

Everyone in the ancient world understood this. Crucifixion was a shameful way to die. It involved the ritualistic and total degradation of the individual. It was a cruel process of public humiliation.

In Middle Eastern culture, of course, a person's honour was of paramount importance. Shame was to be avoided at all costs. To have one's honour questioned or destroyed brought exclusion from community and a desperate isolation. This was true for Greeks, Romans and Jews. For them, honour and shame were critical values. Life was about pursuing honour and eschewing shame. The same was true for the New Testament writers. Their language obeys the grammar of honour and shame as well.

In a world where *philotimia* (the love of honour) was pivotal, death by crucifixion was seen as the ultimate disaster. Here every hint of honour was denied to the victim, who was abused not only physically but verbally too. The victim not only suffered the violent blows of fists and whips, but also had to suffer the shame of taunts and insults.

This is precisely what the Son of God endures for our sakes. He may have scorned this shame (Hebrews 12.2), but he still had to endure it, and in enduring it he suffered not only a sense of separation from *Abba*'s love but also extreme shame at the hands of those who did him violence.

The fury of the orphan

At this point I need to address once again the issue of wrath. Was it really *the Father's* wrath that Jesus experienced, directed at himself, at Calvary?

Let me answer this by describing what happens as orphans grow up.

Often, children separated from their biological parents will experience not just deep grief but also an inner rage. They will be saddened, broken-hearted even, that their parents left them. But they will also feel angry – perhaps furious – that the ones who should have protected and provided for them walked away, leaving them unsafe in a dangerous world.

Feelings of abandonment and rejection therefore create anger in the orphan's heart, which can be unleashed in violent, even criminal, ways. If you don't believe me, look at what Moses did to the Egyptian soldier.

Anyone who has parented an adopted child will know how this rage can show itself. Adoptees, feeling that their biological parents didn't want them, experience a profound sense of being separated and ashamed. However great the adoptive parents are, they now become the target of the child's anger. Without realizing it (most of the time), adoptees seek to project their own feelings of abandonment and rejection onto the parents who have adopted them. In other words, they create circumstances and engage in behaviour designed to make their adoptive parents feel as abandoned, rejected and ashamed as they do. 'I'll make you feel what I feel,' they vow.

In light of this, in my view it is much more appropriate to talk about the rage of the orphan, born of self-loathing and shame, than the rage of the Father at Calvary.

As Jesus experiences the humiliation of crucifixion, with all its physical and verbal violence, he willingly accepts the full weight of our orphan-hearted rage at being separated and ashamed since Eden. He accepts the challenge behind the orphan's fury: 'I'll make you feel what I feel.'

In saying 'yes' to the call to absorb this rage, Jesus does not then say 'no' to the orphan. Rather he refuses to stop loving the orphans who are projecting their wrath onto him. In fact, he forgives them. As orphans, they do not know what they're doing. Their rage is born of their own sense of rejection.

In embracing the shame of the cross, therefore, the Son of God takes vicariously the fury of the orphan. He never hits back, because retaliation is a reflex of the unhealed orphan heart, and rage in the end merely reproduces after its own kind. Instead, he goes on and on loving those who afflict and degrade him, saying through his death what he had conveyed in his life: 'The Father himself loves you dearly.'

The Son who became an orphan

So what has this all got to do with our salvation?

'Everything,' is the answer.

It is often said of theories of the atonement which stress the love of God that they end up making Jesus' death merely an inspiring example.[2] Jesus said, 'Greater love has no one than this: to lay down one's life for one's friends' (John 15.13). Those who say that the death of Jesus is the ultimate demonstration of such love don't go far enough. They turn Jesus' Passion into a moral example, but they fail to explain what has permanently and objectively changed between us and God, and between God and us.

I do not deny that my understanding of the atonement is rooted in my understanding of the Father's love. But this does not mean that I see the Son's death as simply a demonstration of the Father's love. It of course a demonstration; in fact, it is the most graphic and poignant display of divine love within the entire course of human history. But it is also more than that.

Something objective happens at Calvary. Something shifts for ever in the relationship between God and us, and between us and God.

On the cross, the Son of God willingly experiences the full torture of the orphan condition. This condition is the same at both the spiritual level (when applied to all human beings) and the physical level (when applied to literal orphans). It is characterized by separation and shame. On the cross, the Son of God experiences both of these in shocking ways.

In his own body he takes responsibility for the rebellion against the Father's love in every human being, even though he himself has never rebelled against this love. In the process, he endures a temporary sojourn into the far country, amid the rubble of the prodigal, experiencing what life can descend to when one lives apart from *Abba*'s love.

In short, in his human heart he experiences the trauma of separation from the Father's love.

In addition he takes the blows unleashed by the fury of the orphan, who rages against kind and good people without realizing why. Jesus takes this violence on the chin, never retaliating or threatening revenge. He suffers physical and verbal abuse of the worst kind, accepting the call to be publicly humiliated for the sake of an orphaned world.

In short, he embraces a shame within his human heart that was not his, but ours.

If this is true, then we are left with only one conclusion. The death of our perfect older Brother Jesus was not just a demonstration of the Father's great love for his orphaned and lost children. It was also the means by which we have been rescued from our orphaned condition – the means by which we have been redeemed from slavery and adopted into sonship.

In the final analysis, what happened at Calvary was indeed a great and miraculous exchange. *On the cross, the Son of God became an orphan so that we who are orphans might become the sons and daughters of God.*

In his death, Jesus endured our primal orphan wound, experiencing the orphan's worst pain, and uttering the orphan's cry of abandonment. He suffered the condemnation of the enemy and the wrath of the orphan as he died. All this he did to save us, to rescue us from every form of slavery and to restore us to the Father. As the writer to the Hebrews puts it:

> Since the children have flesh and blood, he too shared in their humanity so that by his death he might break the power of him who holds the power of death – that is, the devil – and free those who all their lives were held in slavery by their fear of death. (Hebrews 2.14–15)

This is indeed a mighty exodus.

This is the gospel.

9

A glorious homecoming

The glory of Calvary consists in this: it signalled the beginning of the end for the orphan condition. By taking our sinful rebellion against the Father's love, absorbing it into his own sinless body on the cross, the Son experienced the angst of our orphaned planet. His shout from the cross was accordingly a shout of solidarity – an expression of the empathic oneness he felt in his human heart with the orphan's protest. His lament at the Place of the Skull was the primal scream of the abandoned child who yells for his or her father and mother, a scream that is met by silence. In short, his deepest desolation is for all time the orphan's greatest consolation.

As the body of the Son of God was brought down from the cross, tectonic plates began to move in the foundations of the earth. A mighty shift occurred in which an ancient curse began to be reversed.

As our substitute, Jesus took the full force of the orphan's rage on the cross. He accepted the accumulative wrath of every spiritual orphan, choosing not to retaliate, but to release mercy. And so we were forgiven!

At the same time, he received the condemnation that the law had required. The enemy's power to accuse us was gone. Our seemingly endless debt to the law was cancelled. Our chains fell to the ground. And so we were free!

The death of Jesus was therefore an act of divine kindness. It was the emphatic 'no' of the Father to the agony of our separation and shame. It was his resounding 'yes' to the longing in his heart and ours for reconciliation. As the apostle Paul put it, in what is arguably the finest summary of the *purpose* of the cross in the New Testament: 'God was reconciling the world to himself in Christ, not counting people's sins against them' (2 Corinthians 5.19).

'Reconciliation' – that was the Father's plan. Through his one and only Son, the Father effected a dramatic transformation of the human condition. 'No more orphans!' was his shout from heaven. The Son, picking up the heavy baton of a Roman crossbeam, met the call with unflinching courage and unparalleled love.

The Son died as an orphan so that we who are orphans might become daughters and sons.

Back to the garden

But it wasn't only the crucifixion that brought about our rescue from the orphan condition. The resurrection of Christ was also essential. This is why any theory of the atonement that does not connect the cross with what preceded and succeeded it in Christ's life is deficient. Christ's perfect life of Sonship before his death is a saving life – a life that is part of the Father's rescue plan. Christ's miraculous resurrection from the grave after his death is a saving resurrection – a resurrection that rescues us too.

If we look at John's account, this becomes abundantly clear. In his Gospel, the discovery that Jesus is no longer dead, but alive, occurs in a garden.

Gardens are of course important in the Bible. The trouble had all begun in a garden. In Eden, Adam and Eve had rebelled against the Father and fallen into a dismal state of separation and shame. In an act of kindness, the Father expelled them from the garden before a greater harm befell them. They had already eaten fruit from the tree of knowledge. Had they then eaten from the tree of life – the tree whose fruit is *eternal* life – they would have been perpetually and indeed *eternally* orphaned. In order to put distance between them and this tree, the Father removed his two children from the garden, in the process defusing the possibility of our being for ever orphaned. Far from being a heartless rejection, this was therefore a merciful ejection. Our expulsion was part of the Father's rescue plan, conceived before the fall – before creation itself, in fact. It was his way of saying, 'I will not tolerate my children being eternally orphaned.'

What the Father had in mind of course was the gracious sending of his only Son from heaven. He would live a life of perfect obedience, showing the world what orphans can become if they choose the call to become sons and daughters. He would die a death of perfect obedience, breaking the chains of slavery with which the enemy had bound us since the fall. In his death he would experience the orphan condition vicariously, drinking from the cup of our separation and shame, absorbing our hatred and rage. In short, the immortal Son would taste the mortality of our orphan state.

Three days later, the Father would send the power of the Holy Spirit from heaven. This power would invade the tomb of Jesus, infiltrating every cell of his body, creating a burst of light and life whose radiance was as startling as the one that exploded at the dawn of creation.

The Son would awake, his face aglow with the glory of God, his body transfigured by the life of heaven. He would walk out into the garden, just as the First Adam had, only this time as the serpent's conqueror. As the Last Adam, this heavenly man would therefore undo the devastating damage done at Eden. He would take us from being orphans and, through his death and resurrection, bring us back to *Abba* Father.

The resurrection was accordingly vital for our rescue from the orphan state. As a result of Easter Sunday, we are no longer slaves, bound by the heavy chains of religion. We are the friends of God, liberated into the joy of relating to the Father as his sons and daughters.

Thanks to the risen Son, we can now return to the Father's house and be reconciled to the Love of all loves.

My Father, your Father

Perhaps it is not yet clear how the resurrection of Christ brings about the miraculous deliverance from slavery into sonship.

If so, recall the incident in the garden of the empty tomb. According to John's Gospel, the first person to encounter the risen Son is Mary Magdalene. She meets him in the garden and at first fails to recognize him. In fact she thinks he is the gardener (John 20.15).

Then the stranger calls her by name. 'Mary,' he says.

With that, Mary Magdalene recognizes Jesus. She is overwhelmed with joy and falls upon her Messiah's neck, hugging and holding him out of desperate love.

But Jesus then steps back. 'You can't go on holding me like this,' he says. 'I have not yet ascended to the Father.'

Why does he say this?

It is because, with the resurrection, everything has changed. Jesus will no longer be present in his human body on the earth. He is ascending to the Father. He is returning to heaven. When that happens, God will no longer be embraced in the way that Mary Magdalene is embracing the physically resurrected Son in the garden. He will be embraced through the gift of the Holy Spirit. This gift will cause the hearts of those who receive it to burn with love for the Father and the Son. Filled with the Spirit of adoption, anyone who is in Christ will now be able to approach the Father and embrace him, just as Jesus had prophesied to the Samaritan woman (John 4.23–24).

For Mary Magdalene, then, this means a whole new understanding of what it means to enjoy friendship with Jesus and intimacy with God. She will no longer hold on to the human Messiah. She will adore the Father, who is spirit.

What Mary of Magdala has to learn is therefore a lesson we all have to learn. The death and resurrection of Christ has changed everything in the way in which we relate to God. This is why Jesus tells Mary to go and tell the disciples, 'I am ascending to my Father and your Father' (John 20.17).

Notice the phrase, 'your Father'. This is the risen Lord speaking. He is saying, 'God is my *Abba* and has always been my *Abba*. He will always be my dearest Father.'

But he is saying more than that.

'Thanks to the death I have died and the new life I have received, you can know God as your *Abba* too. You can be freed from slavery into sonship and daughterhood. God can be your *Abba* just as he is mine.'

With the resurrection of Christ, Mary Magdalene has become a daughter of the King.

Vindicated as Son

This brings us to an absolutely critical point about the resurrection of Christ. Thanks to the total obedience of the Son, even to the point of death upon a Roman cross, a new creation has begun within the landscape of our orphaned planet. As at the first creation, something has occurred within a garden. This time, however, the consequences are not disastrous but redemptive. This time, the Last Adam has resisted the enemy, defeated him at Calvary and restored what was lost: the original mandate of sonship and kingship.

The resurrection of Christ therefore initiates the new creation. This re-creative work is the work of the Father, through his Son, in the power of the Holy Spirit. It is a plan that achieves at least two grand purposes.

In the first instance, the Father sends the revivifying power of his Spirit into the tomb in which his dead Son is lying. This energizing power brings heavenly life to Christ's physical body, transforming it into a spiritual body. This metamorphosis is not a denial of human physicality, which is why we see the resurrected Lord eating with his disciples. As the Son is resurrected, his body becomes a glorious, incorruptible and immortal body, one that can dwell in the unapproachable light of the Father's immediate presence. When Jesus Christ is raised from the dead, he is therefore raised for ever. Unlike Lazarus, or the daughter of Jairus, or the son of the widow of Nain, this man will never have to die again. What the Son has experienced no one has experienced. This is permanent resurrection, not temporary resuscitation.

But it is more than that. It is also a vindication.

Keep in mind that some of the contemporaries of Jesus had questioned his right to use language that suggested that he was the Father's Son, that he was somehow one with God, that God was his *Abba*. They had accused him of blasphemy.

But when the Father raised his crucified Son on the first Easter morning, the claims of Christ were upheld and proven. His resurrection was his vindication. It was the startling and unmistakable confirmation of his identity as the one and only Son of God by nature. As Paul states:

> God chose me to be an apostle, and he appointed me to preach the good news that he promised long ago by what his prophets said in the holy Scriptures. This good news is about his Son, our Lord Jesus Christ! As a human, he was from the family of David. But the Holy Spirit proved that Jesus is the powerful Son of God, because he was raised from death.
>
> (Romans 1.1–4 CEV)

Notice the word 'proved'. The resurrection of Christ was the undeniable proof that there was something utterly unique about his identity. That identity consists of this truth: he was and is 'the powerful Son of God'.

Brand-new creations

The first purpose of the Father was accordingly to pour out his Spirit upon the dead body of his Son, bringing about a miraculous new creation and vindicating the claim that Jesus is the *monogenes* of God – the one-of-a-kind, special, precious and unique Son of the living God.

But there's more.

The second purpose was to do something about our identity as followers of the Messiah. As a result of Christ's resurrection, the process that had been under way since the Incarnation reached a history-changing climax. For now it was not just the case that Jesus had died vicariously in our place, embracing the orphan condition in order to redeem us through his blood. It was also the case that Christ in his resurrection had made it possible for us to move beyond the status of 'rescued slaves' to one of 'adopted daughters and sons'. This is why the resurrection of Christ was as important as his crucifixion.

We might put it this way. The events of Good Friday brought us out of slavery in Egypt. The events of Easter Sunday brought us into the promised landscape of our sonship.

It is precisely for this reason that the risen Son says to Mary Magdalene that she can go to the disciples and tell them that he is ascending to 'my Father and your Father'. The third day has brought about a profound transformation in our relationship with God. The Son by nature has enabled us to become sons and daughters by adoption. His God can now be our God. His *Abba* can now be our *Abba* too.

This is why the resurrected Christ says something that at first sight looks strange when he encounters some of his disciples who have gone out fishing with Simon Peter. Jesus appears to the seven of them, standing on the beach of the Sea of Tiberias, while they are in their boat. Notice how the New King James Version (NKJV) picks up the nuance of Jesus' call to them: 'But when the morning had now come, Jesus stood on the shore; yet the disciples did not know that it was Jesus. Then Jesus said to them, "Children, have you any food?" They answered Him, "No"' (John 21.4–5 NKJV).

How does Jesus address his disciples? In most translations he says, 'Friends . . .' But the NKJV gives a more faithful rendering.

Jesus calls out, 'Children . . .' Actually, it is the diminutive of the word 'child' that Jesus uses in the original language. He shouts, 'Little children!'

Why is it that Jesus addresses his disciples like this? It is because he has redeemed them from the slavery of the orphan condition just as he promised he would. But he has also now made it possible for them to become the children of God, the whole purpose behind the work that his Father had given him to do (John 1.12–13).

Thanks to the resurrection of Christ, we are no longer slaves, not even rescued and redeemed slaves. We have a brand-new identity, one befitting brand-new creations. In Christ we are now the adopted children of his Father and ours. Our task is to grow from being little children to children, and from children to mature daughters and sons.

This is the second purpose behind the re-creation begun in the Father's resurrection of his perfect Son.

Rediscovering the Ascension

In light of this, it is imperative not to create an understanding of the cross of Christ that relegates the resurrection to a postscript, or that disconnects Easter Day from Good Friday. In John's Gospel, the crucifixion, resurrection and indeed the Ascension of the Son of God are all part of one unbroken upward movement in which the Son returns home to the Father. They are all part of what John calls 'the hour' of Jesus – the time of his departure from the earth and his elevation to heaven.

This brings us to the much-neglected subject of the Ascension of Christ.

How does Christ's Ascension affect us?

Here we need to remember that Jesus Christ returns to the Father as the Last Adam, and he does so through his suffering on the cross, through his resurrection from the dead, and then finally his Ascension into heaven. This journey home has massive implications for mortal human beings. Just as the First Adam is representative of all human beings in their orphaned state, so the Last Adam is representative of all human beings in their redeemed state. When Jesus is lifted up – in the fullest sense of crucified, raised and ascended to heaven – he rises heavenwards towards the Father's house. The good news – no, the great news – is this. He returns to the Father as the perfect older Brother of every person who has chosen to receive redemption and adoption in Christ. In other words, he blazes the trail from our orphaned planet to the gates of the Father's house, and he takes us in a very real sense with him. In Christ's homecoming we experience our own homecoming.

This act of homecoming (in which Ascension is the climactic moment) is therefore the reverse of the Incarnation.

In the Incarnation, the Son of God came and dwelt in our place, living for 30 years or so on this orphaned planet, embracing the full horror of what it means to be a spiritual orphan when he died on the cross.

In the Ascension, we who were once spiritually orphaned are lifted up in Christ Jesus to the Father's house in heaven, where we can experience the unspeakable joy of what it means to be the royally adopted sons and daughters of God.

To put it in more familiar, traditional language, if the Incarnation means 'God with us', then the Ascension means 'us with God'.

It is here that we can see why the apostle Paul's teaching about being 'in Christ' is so indispensable for understanding our sonship. In Christ, we die to our old rebellion, we rise up out of our slavery, and we come home to be seated in the heavenly realms with Christ Jesus. In Christ we are lifted up by the Holy Spirit into the Son's relationship with his Father in heaven. In Christ, we participate in the invigorating and honoured life of authentic sonship.

As people who live in the legacy of Jesus Christ the Last Adam, we can now embrace our position as sons and daughters by adoption, relating to the Father in love, ruling on the earth with his kindness. All this is because, in Christ's return to the Father, those who were once orphans are now invited home as sons and daughters. Truly, when Christ returned to heaven, he brought many sons and daughters to glory (Hebrews 2.10).

The purpose of the atonement

Perhaps we can see now why theories of the atonement that neglect adoption sell people short. The purpose of Christ's death was not only martial, to defeat the devil. It was not only sacrificial, to die in our place. It was not only commercial, to rescue us from the slave market. Nor was it only legal, to grant us a favourable verdict in the courtroom of heaven. The Father's chief purpose was relational. It was to draw us home into his eternal family. It was to enable us to hear those glorious words: 'This child of mine was lost, but has now been found!' (see Luke 15.24–32). Only if we shift the centre of gravity from the forensic to the filial do we begin to understand this.

The reason why our perfect older Brother came into the orphanage of this earth to rescue us can be summed up in one simple but glorious phrase: *for intimate communion with the triune God*. The rescue mission undertaken by the Son was a mission of adoption. The Father took the initiative. His Son responded to the call and paid the price. His Spirit brings us into the heartfelt reality of our position as sons and daughters of the King of kings.

As such, the story of our spiritual adoption, which is the story of the Bible, is a story about how the three persons of the Trinity rescued us. Just look at what we have been examining in this chapter – the homecoming of the Son. See how the three persons of the Trinity are involved. At every point the Son is carried by the Holy Spirit. He is borne up by the Spirit in the dreadful suffering of the crucifixion. He is resurrected from the dead by the life-giving energy of the Holy Spirit. He is carried by the Spirit at the Ascension, right to the very heart of the Father, where he has always had his home. Likewise, at every point the Father is with him, weeping over his dying Son at the cross, sending the Holy Spirit at the resurrection, receiving his Son home at the Ascension.

The crucifixion, resurrection and Ascension of the Son of God are therefore events in which the whole family of the Trinity is involved. When the Scriptures say that God was reconciling the world to himself, the whole of the Godhead participated. Just as at creation the three persons of the Trinity acted in loving collaboration, so it is at the new creation. The Father, the Son and the Holy Spirit all act together to restore what the First Adam lost. They all participate in ending the orphan plight.

Thanks to the homecoming of the Son, we can therefore now be welcomed home and experience constant and intimate communion with the triune God.

The Father has taken the initiative out of love. In his Son he has secured our adoption. We can now delight to love our heavenly Father because in Christ he first loved us and has now included and enfolded us in the infinite circle of his triune love.

The gift Abba *promised*

In all this the Holy Spirit plays a vital role, not only in the *process* of adoption but in the *appropriation* of it too. In other words, we know that the Holy Spirit was intimately and inextricably involved in the Son's life, death and return to the Father. At every moment, Jesus Christ was empowered and accompanied by the Holy Spirit to achieve all that was necessary in bringing many daughters and sons to glory. At the same time, none of this would be felt by us personally were it not for the fact that the Father and the Son poured out the Holy Spirit on the Day of Pentecost. When that happened, the first disciples were baptized and drenched in *Abba* Father's love and filled with the Spirit of adoption. Their hearts were set ablaze with an unbridled affection for God, whom they could now call *Abba* Father, just as Jesus had in his incarnate life. This was the gift the Father had promised, and it is promised to us too. If we choose to turn from our rebellion and return to the Father, then the Holy Spirit gathers us up into the Son's adoration of the Father, enabling us to cry *'Abba'* from our hearts, and to live as his adopted daughters and sons.

What this shows is that the story of our adoption in Christ cannot bypass the event of Pentecost in the past or the need to be filled with the Spirit of adoption in the present. As Paul makes clear in his Letter to the Romans, those who are led by the Spirit are the children of God. In other words, living the Spirit-filled and the Spirit-directed life is a key hallmark of our sonship (Romans 8.14). To be indwelt by the Spirit of adoption is therefore not an optional extra for mystically minded Christians. It is a prerequisite for all those who are in Christ:

> The Spirit you received does not make you slaves, so that you live in fear again; rather, the Spirit you received brought about your adoption to sonship. And by him we cry, *'Abba, Father.'* The Spirit himself testifies with our spirit that we are God's children.   (Romans 8.15–16)

Paul's words here confirm that what was achieved *objectively* at the cross can only be applied *subjectively* through the Spirit. If the purpose of the cross is familial – restoring lost daughters and sons to their Father in heaven – then this can only be experienced once the Spirit of adoption has captured our hearts. We are not to behave as slaves, living out of a centre of fear. We are to behave as daughters and sons, living out of a centre of love. This can only happen when the same Spirit who secured our adoption in Christ is given full reign within us. Then we too can cry, *'Abba, Father.'*

The problem of course is that too often we have been fearful of the affective dimension to authentic Christian spirituality. Too often we have focused on having light in our heads without warmth in our hearts. This is dangerous.

Whenever we neglect the mystical side of Christianity, we tend to create a moralistic alternative. When that happens, we replace relationship with religion and have nothing but another version of slavery to offer to orphan hearts that are still separated from the Father's love. So we cannot neglect or ignore the gift *Abba* Father promised: the gift of the Holy Spirit.

Somehow we must move beyond a fear and suspicion of experiential Christianity into the life-enhancing atmosphere of the Father's love.

Somehow we must overcome our mistrust of spiritual affections and allow the Spirit of adoption to testify to our spirits that we are the children of God.

Somehow we must allow the perfect love of God to drive out all our fears so that we can have our hearts inflamed with a constant longing to cry out, '*Abba*, Father!'

Somehow we must find a way of being baptized in the Father's love so that we can stand in the river with his Son and hear the words, 'This is my beloved child!'

Beholding the Father

John Owen understood the importance of this very clearly. Writing in the middle of the seventeenth century, he was alarmed at how few Christians had what he called an 'experimental' (what we would call 'experiential') faith. He was particularly worried by the lack of intimacy with the Father:

> How few of the saints are experimentally acquainted with this privilege of holding immediate communion with the Father in love! With what anxious, doubtful thoughts do they look upon God, what fears, what questioning are there, of his good will and kindness! At the best, many think there is no sweetness at all in him towards us, other than that which is purchased at the high price of the blood of Jesus. It is true: that alone is the way of communion; but the free fountain and spring of everything is in the bosom of the Father. So eye the Father as love; look not on him as a lowering father,

but as one most kind and tender. Let us look upon him by faith as one that has had thoughts of kindness towards us from everlasting.[1]

Reading this, it may come as no surprise to hear that Owen was heavily criticized by some of his contemporaries for his mystical sentiments. But it is not for nothing that Owen is described as the 'prince of the Puritans'. Nor would it be without benefit for those who are encouraging a neo-Puritan revival in our times to remember that 'holding immediate communion with the Father in love' was at the heart of all Owen said and did. For him, beholding the Father in love was the normal Christian life. This is precisely why Owen was deeply concerned by the number of 'saints' (that is, Christians) who loved Jesus but who were afraid of the Father. As he put it:

> Christians walk oftentimes with exceedingly troubled hearts, concerning the thoughts of the Father towards them. They are well persuaded of the Lord Jesus Christ and his good will; the difficulty lies in what is their acceptance with the Father – what his heart is towards them.[2]

John Owen was determined that people should experience the Father's love, by which he meant 'the affection of union and nearness'[3] of the Father to us. As soon as the focus of a person changes from the love of the Father to some other attribute, such as God's wrath, then it leads to 'the flying and hiding of sinners'.[4] But 'when he who is the Father is considered as a father, acting with love on the soul, this raises it to love again.'[5] For Owen, then, the Father's love was to be a reality in our hearts, not just a doctrine in our heads.

Receiving our inheritance

To summarize: the big story of the Bible is the story of a loving Father who sends his only Son into the world to rescue his lost children from their orphan state. This dramatic rescue operation reaches its climax in the days that lead from Good Friday to the Day of Pentecost. If Jesus hadn't been lifted up from the cross, lifted up from the grave, lifted up into the heavens, the work of adoption would have been left incomplete. But thanks to our older Brother's death, resurrection and Ascension, everything required for our adoption has been sealed objectively. Thanks to the outpouring of the Spirit of adoption on the Day of Pentecost, we can know *Abba* Father subjectively as we live our lives in Christ, who is the Son of God.

Having said all that, we must realize that there is a limit to the affectionate communion we can enjoy with our *Abba* in this mortal life. Right now, we are clothed in fallen flesh and dwell on this imperfect planet, and as such we do not have face-to-face intimacy with our heavenly Father. We have a communion that is mediated by the Holy Spirit. We operate by faith, and to have faith is to believe in the one you cannot yet see.

But this is not how it will always be.

The Bible promises us that, as soon as we become adopted as sons and daughters of God, we become co-heirs with the Son by nature, Jesus Christ (Romans 8.17).

What did Jesus inherit?

As a result of his obedience, he inherited a glorious, everlasting resurrection body. Those who choose to live as the adopted children of God will receive the same inheritance. One day, when the Son of God returns, we will be raised from death. Then we will see the Father, and he will wipe every tear from our eyes.

In our resurrection bodies, we will no longer enjoy a limited, mediated relationship with *Abba* Father, but rather a limitless, immediate relationship with him. When that day happens, we will receive the reward of our faith, which is to see the one in whom we believed.

So this is the hope of the children of God. This is the future tense of our adoption in Christ. It is the glorious prospect for which we groan daily. As the apostle Paul put it in Romans 8.22–24:

We know that the whole creation has been groaning as in the pains of childbirth right up to the present time. Not only so, but we ourselves, who have the firstfruits of the Spirit, groan inwardly as we wait eagerly for our adoption to sonship, the redemption of our bodies. For in this hope we were saved.

This salvation is not, however, an invitation to passivity. Our Father in heaven never intended us to say, 'I'm pardoned, forgiven and going to heaven', and then do nothing while we wait. He planned the exact opposite for us. As we will see in the final chapter, his plan was never that we would be saved enough to go to heaven when we die. It was always for us to be saved enough to bring heaven to earth while we live.

For the adopted daughter or son of God, there is therefore a great mission to be accepted and an epic adventure to be embraced in this present life. It will require us to accept the call to suffer, as our perfect older Brother did. But it will also mean that we experience the glory of God appearing in our lives as heaven invades earth.

I cannot think of anything more challenging or more exhilarating than that.

10

The heart of the gospel

Several years ago a young man asked if he could visit me. He was the leader of a nationwide Christian youth movement in the UK. He had read some of my books about the Fatherhood of God, spiritual adoption and the healing of the orphan heart, and he wanted to ask me some questions.

When he arrived I was impressed by his love for young people and his earnest and genuine longing for the millions of teens in the UK to understand and respond to the good news. He was clearly a man with a vision for bringing the gospel to the youth culture in Britain's cities.

The conversation went something like this.

'I've read your books on the Father's love,' he said, 'and I can't help thinking that what you describe is a vital key for this generation.'

I asked him to explain.

'The thousands of young people that we serve in the urban contexts of this country don't understand the traditional version of the gospel message.'

'What do they find difficult?' I asked.

'They can't relate to the picture of God as an angry judge, and us as condemned sinners,' he replied.

'So how do you present the gospel?'

'That's why I'm here,' he replied. 'I believe that the primary problem in contemporary youth culture is fatherlessness. Kids just don't have dads any more. They're looking for substitute fathers and families in gangs.'

'So how has that affected the way you evangelize young people?' I asked.

'This is where we need help,' he said. 'I'm convinced that somehow we must tell them that God is the most loving dad in the universe and that he sent his Son to bring them home. The question is how we go about this.'

'A lot of work still has to be done,' I answered, 'but the key is first to realign our image of God to what Jesus taught about the Father, and then to rediscover the lost doctrine of adoption.'

'That's what we're trying to do in our organization,' he said.

'Well, it won't be too long before you find the answer,' I replied, 'because what you're talking about is the message of the Father's love. That is not just the message of the hour. It's the heart of the gospel.'

A neglected jewel

If we are to communicate the good news in an effective way in the twenty-first century, then, we will need to return to one of the greatest insights that the apostle Paul ever had about the cross of Christ, which is that it is the means by which human beings are rescued from slavery and restored to true sonship. In other words, we will need to rediscover the lost jewel of spiritual adoption.

And it *is* a lost jewel.

When in the 1990s I researched my book *From Orphans to Heirs*,[1] subtitled *Celebrating our spiritual adoption*, I looked for other books devoted to our adoption in Christ. I was astonished by how few there were. In the entire course of Western church history, this doctrine – which is every bit as biblical as 'justification', 'redemption' and 'regeneration' – seems to have been strangely neglected.

Since the publication of *From Orphans to Heirs*, however, there has been a steady stream of related works, especially from Trevor Burke, whose books *Adopted into God's Family* (2006) and *The Message of Sonship* (2011) have helped to fill the gap.[2] But prior to 1999, when my book was published, the shelves were almost empty.

To some degree, this neglect has human causes. The German Reformer Martin Luther, for example, had a notoriously poor relationship with his earthly father. It is well known that he found it difficult to recite the beginning of the Lord's Prayer ('Our Father in heaven') because, every time he did, he thought of his own father who was cruel and aloof. This is at least one major reason why his theology became more legal than relational in character. In Luther's eyes, God is a perfect judge and we are all of us in the wrong, but Christ, who was completely in the right, took the punishment for our sins, dying in our place, so that we could be declared 'not guilty' and clothed in the righteousness of Christ.

This legal or juridical story, deriving from a law-based view of God, took root in many of the Western churches and led for centuries to a neglect of the Father heart of God and his unceasing love for spiritual orphans, a love that took his Son to the cross. The legacy of the Reformation was therefore one that gave priority to justification over adoption, to the legal over the filial. For a long time this seemed bizarre to me, given the emphasis that the adoption metaphor enjoys, not just in Paul's letters but in the overarching story of the Bible.

It appeared to me that one of the few times when the doctrine of spiritual adoption momentarily surfaced in the Western Church was during seasons of revival. It may come as no surprise, then, that John Wesley often preached on this subject, and Romans 8.15 was one of his favourite passages.[3] But other than during such times of revival, the priceless truth of our adoption out of slavery into sonship was usually only a footnote to justification.

Today, having come to the realization that the devil is the original orphan, I know the explanation is not hard to find. The neglect of the Father's love has more than just a human cause. There is a demonic strategy behind it all. The enemy is determined that we should not discover that God is Father and so he has been causing havoc in the relationships between fathers and their children worldwide. The fatherlessness in the earth today, which has reached pandemic proportions, is ultimately his doing. He is desperate for people to be so wounded by their fathers that it becomes nigh on impossible for them to call God '*Abba* Father'. He wants human beings to remain in slavery, whether that is to legalism or hedonism. What he doesn't want is Christians who know that they are the adopted daughters and sons of God. He is determined to stop men and women from understanding their identity and receiving their inheritance in Christ. So he casts a veil over people's minds, and this in turn leads to the neglect of the Father heart of God and the liberating doctrine of adoption.

A persecuted message

Observe what happens on those rare occasions in the Western Church when someone tries to restore the Fatherhood of God and the beauty of our spiritual adoption to their rightful place of emphasis.

Right now, I cannot help thinking of one of the greatest theologians in Scottish church history, John McLeod Campbell – the biggest influence on the mind of the twentieth-century theologian Professor T. L. Torrance. Torrance's younger brother James wrote the Introduction to Campbell's magnificent book *The Nature of the Atonement*, which Campbell published in 1856.[4]

In his Introduction, James Torrance sets the historical scene for the development of Campbell's unique theology. The Scottish Church in the 50 years during which Campbell worked (from the 1820s to the 1870s) was dominated by an extreme form of Calvinism in which people's basic concept of God was that of a lawgiver (understood in terms of Western jurisprudence). Their view of the atonement was therefore a legal one. God the Lawgiver had declared that human beings were guilty of breaking the law and that the sentence for this crime was death. However, Christ came into the world to satisfy the conditions of God's law. On the cross he appeased God's wrath, and his shed blood provided the conditions by which grace could be extended to the elect. This theology, James Torrance argues, led to people believing that God is a contract-God, not a covenant-God; that the atonement is limited, not universal in scope; and that the judicial is more important than the filial.

It was within this landscape that Campbell grew up as the son of a minister. Early on in his childhood, Campbell's mother died. However, his father not only carried on his work as a minister but brought up his children with extraordinary devotion and affection. Indeed, later in his life Campbell was to say he filled the word 'father' with meaning.

In light of his own father's love, it is no surprise that Campbell, having trained for the ordained ministry, should preach about the Father heart of God and our spiritual adoption. Appointed to the parish of Rhu in Dunbartonshire, Campbell was quickly distressed by the lack of assurance among his church members. Few if any seemed to be sure of the Father's kindness and love towards them. Most of them lived in fear of God as a lawgiving judge. So for the next five years Campbell taught his congregation that God is the most kind and loving of fathers and that his Son came into the world, not to satisfy God's wrath, but to provide a way home for his lost and orphaned children. The benefits of the cross are therefore primarily relational more than legal, and universal (for everyone), not limited (for the elect alone).

This teaching, so unusually focused on the Father heart of God, had two effects. On the positive side it led Campbell's 300 or so parishioners into the joyful assurance of sonship, which was brought about through Campbell's unrelenting emphasis on adoption over justification. On the negative side it caused the church leaders of his denomination to bring charges against him. Their accusation consisted of a complaint that Campbell was teaching that the atonement is universal (for all) and that experiencing assurance is a necessary part of our salvation in Christ. For these two heresies (as they saw it then) he was brought before the Presbytery three times during the year of 1831.

The nature of the atonement

Perhaps the most moving moment in the trials of John McLeod Campbell was when his own doting father appeared as a character witness. Standing before the Presbytery, he fearlessly announced: 'While I live I shall never be ashamed to be the father of so holy and blameless a son. Indeed, in this respect, I challenge anyone in this house to bring forward anyone who can come into competition with him.' Here a father's love was brought into the courtroom context and put on poignant display. That, of course, was a picture of what Campbell himself was trying to do. He was attempting to bring the revelation of the Father's love into a setting dominated by a legal theology. But this irony was lost on Campbell's accusers. In May 1831, the General Assembly deposed him from his ministry.

Twenty-seven years later, Campbell published *The Nature of the Atonement*, one of the greatest works ever to be written on the cross. Here Campbell articulated in great depth and eloquence, in a style that is more devotional than academic, the gospel for which he had been charged and deposed. For him, any preaching of the gospel that left Christians with a feeling of not 'being good enough', of not having a true assurance of God's love, was severely deficient. It left people looking inwards when they should have been gazing upwards.

Campbell's starting point was therefore the character of God as revealed in Jesus Christ. This character is not primarily judicial – as the proponents of the extreme Calvinism of his own day were arguing – but paternal. God's nature, he said, is primarily that of a loving Father. From this view of 'the Fatherly heart of God', Campbell proceeds to give priority to the filial over the judicial. The gospel is not primarily about Christ securing our pardon, but about Christ securing our adoption as daughters and sons. This is entirely consistent with an understanding of God's 'fatherliness'.

Writing with a pastor's heart, Campbell therefore sought to turn his readers' attention away from themselves to the glorious love of their heavenly Father. In the process he succeeded in transforming many people from being slaves to a fear of the Lawgiver to sons and daughters who rested in the certain love of their Father. He did this by making the gospel what it was always designed to be: good news! For Campbell, the fundamental truth about God is that he is our loving Father. The blessing that comes from accepting the gospel is 'following God as dear children walking in love'.[5]

In Campbell's theology, then, the real miracle brought about by believing the gospel message is the transformation of a rebellious orphan into a loving child. That requires a 'miracle of Almighty power' because it causes us to love the Father where we didn't before.[6] Like John Owen before him, Campbell saw the key to this as contemplating the Father in love. When the gospel is preached from this 'contemplation', human beings are granted the '*experience of orphans who have found their long lost Father*'.[7] As a result, sonship is quickened in their hearts, and the misery of their orphan state is ended.

For Campbell, then, the result of hearing and accepting the good news is that human beings have 'an immediate direct confidence in God's fatherly heart'.[8] They enjoy a sense of perpetual, divine acceptance. That being the case, two things become non-negotiable in Campbell's mind. The first is that 'we must *come to God as sons, or not come at all*'.[9] The second is that 'assuredly that word from heaven – "this is my beloved Son, in whom I am well pleased . . ." – each man . . . is called to hear as a word addressed to himself'.[10]

For Campbell, this is the gospel. In his eyes, the good news is not only a matter of us being saved from the condemnation of the law. It is a matter of us being saved to a life of sonship. His contemporaries had greatly neglected this truth and placed the legal over the relational. His predecessors, especially Martin Luther and Jonathan Edwards (both of whom he quotes), had done the same.

Campbell's charge to the Church of his day was therefore to preach the true gospel and the whole gospel. This meant showing 'newly awakened sinners' that God is their loving Father. Indeed, Campbell urged, 'We cannot too soon present the Father to them.'[11] It also meant that every preacher of the gospel was to help his hearers to attain what Campbell called 'the highest form of faith' – 'a faith which is the fellowship of the Son's apprehension of the Father . . . and utters itself in the cry, Abba, Father.'[12]

This gospel message, Campbell stated, leads people into 'the everlasting arms of the Eternal Love'.[13]

Re-imagining the gospel

Given that any attempt to redefine the gospel as a Father message is often attacked, I want to stress in these final pages that this is not a departure from the biblical approach to mission but a radical realignment to it. As the adopted children of God, it is our duty and indeed our joy to look at how our older Brother engaged in his Father's mission, bringing the good news of the kingdom of heaven into the lives of the spiritual orphans all around him. What we discover as we do is that the Son of God by nature – to whose image we are called to be conformed – engaged in a love-based way of communicating the good news, one in other words that was completely rooted in the Father's love. All that I am proposing, therefore, is a simple realignment to the Son's way of spreading the gospel.

Look at John's Gospel. Chapter 4 contains within it the most complete picture we have of how Jesus went about drawing people into the orbit of the Father's love. Much could be said about this chapter, but I will restrict myself to three main characteristics of the way in which Jesus communicated the gospel.

The first was through *mercy*.

At the start of the chapter (verses 1–15), Jesus engages in conversation with a Samaritan woman at a well just outside the town of Sychar. She is astonished that he, a Jewish man, should be talking to her, a Samaritan woman. Jewish men despised Samaritan women, calling them 'dirty from the cradle'. Jewish men were supposed to withdraw 20 paces to avoid them.

But Jesus stays put, and asks her for a drink. This is a picture in miniature of his meal tables. His meals, as I wrote earlier, were always open to those excluded by the religious elite of his day. His table was like King David's, a table of kindness where orphans could be transformed into princes. What Jesus is doing here is revealing the mercy of his Father. He gives the woman embrace, not exclusion.

That brings me to the second way in which Jesus communicated the gospel, and that was through a *message*.

As the two continue to talk (verses 16–26), Jesus tells the woman that she has been married five times and that the man she's now living with is not her husband. This knowledge comes to Jesus directly from his Father, through one of the gifts of the Holy Spirit. This gift is instantly recognized by the Samaritan woman who says, 'Sir, I can see that you are a prophet.'

At this point, the conversation could have gone in an entirely different direction. Had Jesus prioritized the legal operating system – a system in which God is primarily a lawgiver – then it would almost certainly have turned to the woman's secret life of sin and the ways in which she had broken God's law. But this is not how the conversation goes. Jesus instead turns to the subject of his heavenly Father. He talks to her about this loving *Abba* in heaven and excites her with the invitation to become one of the worshippers whom this Father is seeking. As he does, he uses a word that in its Greek translation means literally 'to approach in order to kiss someone' (*proskunein*, to worship).

See how different this is from the traditional gospel message in the Western Church. This is not a message about law but a message about love. This is not a message focused on past failures but on future purpose. This is not a message about religion but about relationship.

133

'God is your perfect Father,' is the message. 'Everything you're looking for in men's arms you will find only in his. He's calling you to draw near and worship him, in Spirit and in truth.' This, then, is a Father message. And the Father message is the gospel.

But this isn't all. Jesus not only communicates the gospel through mercy and through a message. He also uses *miracles*.

This brings us to the end of John 4, to a cameo that is often neglected because of the long and exciting story of the Samaritan woman that precedes it. In this brief incident (verses 43–54), a royal official approaches Jesus with his entire entourage. Jesus hasn't much time for the people who have come with the man. They are only interested in seeing a miracle. Jesus rounds on them and tells them that unless they see signs and wonders they will never believe.

With the royal official, however, Jesus takes a very different approach. This man is a dad, and his boy back home is very sick – close to death even. 'Sir, come down before my child dies,' the man pleads.

'Go, your son will live,' Jesus replies.

What is happening here? Why does Jesus perform a miracle after he has rebuked the man's entourage for always hankering after charismatic sensations?

It is because the man speaks as a father. Something in the heart of Jesus responds to this. In the intimacy of the Trinity, the human heart of the Son of God, joined by the Spirit – the bond of love – to the divine heart of his Father, makes intercession: 'Does this sound familiar?'

'It does, my Son,' the Father whispers.

The royal father's tearful love for his dying son is more than familiar. It is something that has irresistible traction within the triune family. For what will Calvary involve if it is not the most royal of fathers weeping over his dying son?

And so the miracle-working power of God is activated by the Father's empathy, transmitted through the Son's compassion, and wrought through the Spirit's power:

The man took Jesus at his word and departed. While he was still on the way, his servants met him with the news that his boy was living. When he enquired as to the time when his son got better, they said to him, 'Yesterday, at one in the afternoon, the fever left him.'

Then the father realised that this was the exact time at which Jesus had said to him, 'Your son will live.' So he and his whole household believed.   (John 4.50–53)

The power of divine kindness

I have a growing and unquenchable conviction that this three-dimensional approach that Jesus uses – involving mercy, message and miracles – is going to become more and more critical and indeed normative in the communication of the gospel in our fatherless world.

Mercy is going to be essential. This is because the Spirit-led exercise of subversive embrace over and against simplistic exclusion is always a revelation of the Father's love. Every time Christians behave like Jesus did, they demonstrate *Abba*'s merciful heart, and in the process the walls that divide people and nations come crashing down. Every time we open up our meal table to an alienated other, heaven invades earth.

The message is also going to be essential. The creative retelling of the story of an extravagantly loving Father will be the central theme of the good news that we are called to tell in future years. Just as Jesus exercised charismatic creativity in his story of the outrageously kind dad in Luke 15, so we will be given the ability to locate and narrate brand-new parables of the Father's love.

This will not just be restricted to the pulpit either. It will be released through movie-makers and musicians, painters and poets, dancers and dramatists.

Then there are the miracles. Genuine miracles, such as the instant cure of a dying child, are also demonstrations of the kingdom of heaven – of the life-transforming presence of the Father. No one can afford to dismiss the miraculous if they want to reach this fatherless world. Miracles tell a person, '*Abba* Father knows you and loves you dearly.'

Whenever a lost spiritual orphan is on the receiving end of a mercy like this, a message like this, a miracle like this, it can be utterly overwhelming. Brought up in a fatherless world, men and women suddenly realize that they have a Father in heaven even if they don't have a father on earth. They understand, however intuitively, that this Father is not excluding or rejecting them as so many earthly dads do, but revealing a kindness quite unlike anything this world has to offer.

It is this kindness, not God's anger, that causes them to turn their face towards the Father's house. As the apostle Paul said, 'the kindness of God leads you to repentance' (Romans 2.4 NASB).

Coming home to the Father

What then is repentance?

In the Jewish tradition, the word 'repentance' is rendered by the Hebrew term *teshuvah*. In a fascinating and eloquent article on the meaning of *teshuvah*, the former British Chief Rabbi, Jonathan Sacks, has explained the rich nuances of this word in Jewish history and tradition.[14]

In Jewish tradition, it is your duty to confess a sin once it has been committed. 'When a man or woman shall commit any sin that men commit, to do a trespass against the LORD, and that person be guilty; Then they shall confess their sin which they have done' (Numbers 5.6–7 AV). This confession needs to be expressed in words. So the penitent says, 'I beseech you, O Lord, I have sinned, I have acted perversely, I have transgressed before you and have done such and such, and I repent and am ashamed of my deeds, and I will never do this again.'

If this is what confession means, then how is repentance understood?

One tradition is articulated by Maimonides, the great medieval Jewish philosopher, who rooted the idea of *teshuvah* or repentance in the Temple cult in Jerusalem. When the Temple was still standing, sacrifices for sin were brought to the altar. Part of the sacrifice involved a verbal confession, known as the *vidui*, on the part of the penitent individual. The person showed genuine remorse for his or her wrongdoing and made a resolution never to do it again. This represents one tradition.

However, the Temple in Jerusalem was destroyed in AD 70. So the question arises: how did the Jewish people understand and exercise *teshuvah* once the Temple and its sacrifices were no longer part of their everyday life?

Here Nachmanides (a leading Jewish scholar of the Middle Ages) provides an answer. One of the warnings that God gives in the Torah concerns the consequences Israel will have to face if it persists in transgression. The direst result will be exile. The people of God will be dispersed and displaced, scattered over the earth. The only way their fortunes will be reversed is through *teshuvah*, repentance. Turning to God will lead to returning to the land.

The consequence of sin is therefore that we find ourselves in the wrong place, alienated from God, distanced from where we are supposed to be. In other words, we find ourselves far from home. In this second tradition, then, *teshuvah* means coming home. It means moving from exile to return, an action that has both spiritual and physical ramifications.

What we have here is a distinction between two understandings of repentance. The first is a priestly definition, based on the Temple sacrifices, and focused on wrongdoing and guilt. The second is a prophetic definition, based on the story of Israel's exile and return, and focused on alienation and shame.

There is no doubt that both of these interpretations are rooted in the Hebrew Scriptures. But in Western Christianity it would be fair to say that the priestly understanding has had far more air time than the prophetic. The prophetic understanding of repentance as homecoming, as turning from what in Luke 15 Jesus calls the far country and returning to the Father's house, has by and large been ignored. Coming to Jesus, who is the perfect sacrifice for sin, and confessing one's guilt has been understood as the essence of repentance.

Both of these are dimensions of repentance. However, if we continue to emphasize only the priestly understanding of repentance (as verbal confession for sinful things that we have done) and neglect the prophetic understanding (as coming home to the place of honour), we will not help people to respond to the gospel in an integrated way. We will help them to deal with their guilt, but we will not help them to deal with their shame.

As a result, men and women will feel forgiven for what they have done, but they will not feel free from the shame of who they are. They will receive a pardon for sin, but they will not enter into their true position in Christ. For that to happen, sinners need to come home into the Father's house, wearing their robe and their ring (see Luke 15).

When the gospel of the Father's love is preached, we must try to be intentional about helping people to confess verbally where they have rebelled against the Father's love and chosen to live at a distance from the Father, far from home. In other words, we must help people to acknowledge their separation from their adoring *Abba* Father and the alienation they have chosen as the existential norm for their lives. This is as important as the confession of wrong things they have done, including the failure to fulfil the Golden Rule – to love God with the whole of their being and their neighbour as themselves. For the gospel challenge is not only to help people to receive relief from their guilt, but also to know freedom from their shame.

The healing of our shame

I started this book with a story about my adoptive father, so it seems only appropriate that I should end this final chapter with another episode from his life.

My adoptive father served behind enemy lines in General Wingate's army in Burma during the Second World War. After a fierce battle he was captured, imprisoned and tortured by the Japanese army. The suffering he endured was indescribable.

Yet when I was growing up in my father's house, I was constantly warned against being bitter against the Japanese people. In fact, Dad asked me to read a short story by Laurens van der Post about a British soldier who forgave a condemned Japanese sergeant during the war trials after 1945.

'I want you to learn from this story,' Dad said. 'Don't bear grudges. Always forgive.'

I have tried to live by that ever since.

In light of this it seems appropriate to me to refer to what Norman Kraus discovered during the 1980s and 1990s when he tried as a Mennonite missionary to present the gospel to the Japanese people.[15] He discovered that the traditional Western message, focused on how Christ paid the penalty for our sins required by God, made no sense at all. Kraus soon realized that if the Japanese were even to begin to understand this Western gospel, he would have to introduce them to the Western mindset, so focused on guilt and forgiveness, and then persuade them to adopt it in place of their Far Eastern way of thinking, which is focused on shame and honour.

Thankfully, Kraus decided to listen and learn from the Japanese culture. He learned how to present the gospel using the categories of shame and honour, showing how the Son's voluntary and vicarious acceptance of our alienation brought us out of shame and into a great and unmerited honour in the Father's house. In the process, he discovered that he was truer than he ever had been to the spirit of the New Testament, which was forged within a similar context, a culture of honour.

As Kraus began to explore ways of communicating the gospel, he discovered that the most effective approach involved emphasizing how, at the cross, Jesus Christ accepted the call to endure extreme shame. Jesus Christ died a death that involved public degradation, humiliation and alienation. He died naked and outside the city, an outcast and an outsider. He did this out of extreme love, identifying with our shame throughout his whole life (in his love for the marginalized) and especially in his death on the cross. In short, Jesus suffered shameful exclusion in our place and for our sakes.

At the heart of this Far Eastern gospel, the message is this: the Son embraced shame at the cross so that our shame could be removed. Out of great love, he bore the worst degradation and exclusion imaginable so that we could have our shame healed and our honour restored. To use the language that I have introduced and explored in this book, we were in the far country, living as orphans in the pig pen, separated and ashamed, but the Father out of his divine compassion covered our shame with his robe of honour, and restored us to the noble place of sonship.

Jesus therefore didn't just deal with our guilt; he removed our shame. He despised the shame of the cross (Hebrews 12.2), and as a result, his wounds heal our wounds. When the gospel of the Father's love is proclaimed, not only do people receive forgiveness for what they've done. They also receive healing for what and who they are. The gospel is accordingly a message of extraordinary and indeed unparalleled power. It brings redemption from slavery and adoption into sonship.

It deals with our guilt and it heals our shame. No longer are we orphans, separated and ashamed. We are the adopted sons and daughters of God. We live in mystical union with Christ, invited and included into the unending flow of love within the family of the holy and undivided Trinity.

Like the four children at the end of C. S. Lewis's novel *The Lion, the Witch and the Wardrobe*, we wear crowns and sit on thrones, given the right to relate to the Lion and to rule in Narnia.

This is good news for the Japanese.

It is good news for the youth of the UK.

It is good news for orphans.

It is good news for the whole of Creation.

Epilogue

Why did my father shed those tears when he heard that I had earned a place to read English at university?

I have spent a long time trying to answer that question. Today I have an idea.

My adoptive father, Philip Stibbe, loved English literature. He had studied under C. S. Lewis as an undergraduate at Merton College, Oxford. Every Tuesday night during term time he would be invited, along with a handful of other star pupils, to dine with Lewis and discuss literature, politics, philosophy and faith.

Literature was Dad's life. In fact, when he was a prisoner of war, literature had saved his life. Returning to Oxford for his final year after being freed, he left to take up teaching English at Bradfield College, which he did faithfully for over a quarter of a century.

Looking back to that moment when he sat upon the stairs and cried, I now believe that the reason he did that was because he had a dream for my life, a dream of following in his footsteps, a dream of loving literature, a dream of writing books, a dream of teaching other people to love and do the same.

When I was a young boy he heard that I had begun to enjoy the Sherlock Holmes stories. Unknown to me, he went to Blackwell's bookshop in Oxford and bought the complete works of Sir Arthur Conan Doyle in hardback. When they arrived he picked them up, brought them home and gave them to me as a gift when he said goodnight one bedtime.

He clearly had hopes for his adopted son. He wanted me to love the things he loved. But he wasn't going to control or coerce me. His approach was to wait until I showed a spark of enthusiasm, to lay dry wood beneath that tiny flame, and watch with glinting eyes as the fire began to roar.

So that was what lay behind his tears. When he had taken me in his arms in the orphanage all those years before, he had done so because he wanted to give me a chance in life, to expose me to opportunities that I would never have had otherwise, to position me in a landscape of hope where dreams can come true.

What a man he was! And what a picture this is. For what is true of me is true of all of us.

We have an adoptive Father in heaven. In Christ his beloved Son he has rescued us from our orphanage and drawn us home into his arms of love. He too has a dream for us. He longs for us to love what he loves. He wants us to participate in his passion.

So what is our Father's passion?

It is contained within Romans 8.19: 'The creation waits in eager expectation for the children of God to be revealed.' The Father's greatest longing is the deep yearning of our fallen planet. It is for human beings to rise up from their fallen, orphaned state and to embrace their honoured position as adopted daughters and sons.

This is not a privatized enterprise. It is a quest to be undertaken in the community of faith, or better still, in the *family* of God.

When we choose to turn our hearts towards the Father and believe in the Son, then we no longer think with the independent mindset of the orphan. We think 'family' because we recognize that we are adopted into the family of God on earth and the triune family in heaven. This adoption is marked by baptism – an outward act that celebrates the internal journey from our old life of slavery to our new life of sonship and daughterhood. It is continually reinforced through the Lord's Supper, a meal rooted in the Passover story in which the Israelites were rescued from servitude in Egypt to sonship in the promised land. These acts are done in community, not isolation.

As members of the family of God, together as adopted brothers and sisters in Christ, we are called to receive all the benefits of the cross and to rest in our honoured position as God's adopted daughters and sons. But rest does not mean inactivity. The world, the whole Creation in fact, is pining for the followers of Christ to

142

rise up in their true identity, embracing their true destiny, working with their sleeves rolled up to bring heaven to earth.

The cosmos is therefore not pining for the appearance of religious slaves. It is pining for the revelation of the liberated sons and daughters of God. And it is pining because deep down within the groans of the earth there is a sigh of recognition that, when the sons and daughters of God start appearing, their freedom will bring freedom to Creation too.

When believers start to enter into the fullness of their spiritual adoption, no longer bound by the chains of religion but emancipated into love-based holiness, even the environment will be transformed.

The long hard winter will come to an end.

The vines will begin to blossom.

The harvests will be plentiful.

Rivers will be cleansed.

Racism will come to an end.

Slave trafficking will be crushed.

And orphans will find a home.

This is our true inheritance. We must seize it!

And when we begin to move into the reality of *Abba*'s dream, we will look up with joy and feel drops falling upon our faces, like sweet spring rain.

Notes

1 The gospel of the heart

1 P. G. Stibbe, *Return via Rangoon* (London: Leo Cooper / Pen and Sword, 1994). Original edition published in 1947.

2 William Wordsworth, 'Lines Composed a Few Miles above Tintern Abbey . . . July 13, 1798'.

3 Mark Stibbe, *The Drawing Out of Days: A selection of poetry* (OM Publications, 1978).

4 See for example *From Orphans to Heirs: Celebrating our spiritual adoption* (Oxford: Bible Reading Fellowship, 1999). Also my book *The 100 Verse Bible: The essence of the world's most powerful book* (Oxford: Monarch, 2010).

5 See Romans 8.14–17; 8.23; 9.4; Galatians 4.4–7; Ephesians 1.4–5. The noun *huiothesia* is used in all five of these texts. It is translated 'adoption' and literally means 'the placing of a person in the position of a son'.

6 John Updike, *My Father's Tears and Other Stories* (New York: Random House, 2010).

2 Tears from heaven

1 J. B. Phillips, *The New Testament in Modern English* (London: HarperCollins, 1962), copyright © J. B. Phillips, 1958, 1960, 1972.

2 Mark Stibbe, *I Am Your Father: What every heart needs to know* (Oxford: Monarch, 2010). This is a handbook of healing. If you suffer from father-wounds, I suggest you start with this and then read my book *The Father You've Been Waiting For: Portrait of a perfect dad* (Milton Keynes: Authentic, 2006).

3 The passion of the Father

1 For a defence of penal substitutionary atonement (PSA), see Steve Jeffries, Mike Ovey and Andrew Sach, *Pierced for Our Transgressions: Rediscovering the glory of penal substitution* (Nottingham: IVP, 2007).

2 See for example N. T. Wright, 'The Cross and the Caricatures' (Easter 2007) and the response of the authors of *Pierced for Our Transgressions*, 'Response to Wright from the authors of *Pierced for Our Transgressions*'; both articles are available online, <http://www.virtueonline.org/cross-and-caricatures-tom-wright> and <http://thegospelcoalition.org/blogs/justintaylor/2007/04/24/response-to-wright-from-authors-of/>.

3 From Stuart Townend and Keith Getty, 'In Christ Alone', copyright © 2001 Thankyou Music.

4 See online article, 'Keith Getty on What Makes "In Christ Alone" Accepted and Contested', <http://thegospelcoalition.org/article/keith-getty-on-what-makes-in-christ-alone-beloved-and-contested>. The comment quoted here is from Mary Louise Bringle, made to the *Christian Century*, 1 May 2013.

5 See N. T. Wright, 'The Cross and the Caricatures': 'The biblical doctrine of God's wrath is rooted in the doctrine of God as the good, wise and loving creator, who hates – yes, hates, and hates implacably – anything that spoils, defaces, distorts or damages his beautiful creation, and in particular anything that does that to his image-bearing creatures. If God does not hate racial prejudice, he is neither good nor loving. If God is not wrathful at child abuse, he is neither good nor loving. If God is not utterly determined to root out from his creation, in an act of proper wrath and judgment, the arrogance that allows people to exploit, bomb, bully and enslave one another, he is neither loving, nor good, nor wise.'

6 Here's Tom Wright again in 'The Cross and the Caricatures': 'We must of course grant that many Christians have spoken, in effect, of the angry God upstairs and the suffering Jesus placating him. Spoken? They've *painted* it: many a mediaeval altarpiece, many a devotional artwork, have sketched exactly that. And of course for some late mediaeval theologians this was the point of the Mass: God was angry, but by performing this propitiatory sacrifice once more, the priest could make it all right. And it was at least in part in reaction against this understanding of the Eucharist that the Reformers rightly insisted that what happened on the cross happened once for all. They did not invent, they merely adapted and relocated, the idea of the propitiation of God's wrath through the death of Jesus. We must of course

145

acknowledge that many, alas, have since then offered more caricatures of the biblical doctrine.'

7 This is the point that Steve Chalke was trying to make with his co-author Alan Mann in *The Lost Message of Jesus* (Grand Rapids, MI: Zondervan, 2003). Steve is an evangelist who spends much of his time with people who don't hold to a Christian worldview. He was accordingly interceding for them when he and Alan Mann wrote on page 182 the now notorious comments: 'The fact is that the cross isn't a form of cosmic child abuse – a vengeful Father, punishing his Son for an offence he has not even committed. Understandably, both people inside and outside of the Church have found this twisted version of events morally dubious and a huge barrier to faith. Deeper than that, however, is that such a concept stands in total contradiction to the statement that "God is Love". If the cross is a personal act of violence perpetrated by God towards humankind but borne by his Son, then it makes a mockery of Jesus' own teaching to love your enemies and to refuse to repay evil with evil.'

8 The view that God suffers with his creatures has become associated in recent decades with process theology and open theism. But a commitment to saying, 'The Father feels our pain', does not require us to sign up to either of these theological positions. While we cannot simplistically assume that what is true of our emotions is true of God, the fact is that God at the very least has embraced human emotions in his Son. The Incarnation is our key here. In becoming fully human, God in Christ has experienced our emotional life. So whether or not God experiences emotions in the way we do in his *divine nature*, the truth is that he has embraced this reality in the Incarnation, in Christ's *fully human nature*. After the Incarnation, at the very least God suffers with us and he suffers like us. How this sits with the classical theistic view of God's eternal immutability and impassibility continues of course to be debated.

4 A story of adoption

1 Mark Stibbe, *The Father You've Been Waiting For: Portrait of a perfect dad* (Milton Keynes: Authentic, 2006). When I wrote this, my intention was to provide a book that could be placed in the hands of those who are not Christians but who are deep down longing

to discover that God is the world's best Father. The king to whom I was speaking had lost his own father when he was in his teens. The religion of his people was essentially a form of African animism. Using the story of my adoptive father, who became a father figure to him too, I was able to introduce the king to the fatherly love of the one true God, revealed in Jesus. I was also moved to challenge him with the Father's call upon the kings of the Old Testament to love and care for the fatherless. That he took this to heart is confirmed by the fact that several years later he made a royal visit to the Ugandan orphanage whose leaders I had brought with me to the audience. From this testimony alone we can see something of the power of the good news of the Father's love.

2 See Sereno Dwight, *A Life of President Edwards*, vol. 1 (New York, 1830). The material there is said to be taken from a lost manuscript, written by Sarah Edwards herself, entitled *Her Uncommon Discoveries of the Divine Perfections and Glory; and of the Excellency of Christ* (written between 1710 and 1758). Much of Sarah Edwards' story revolves around her longing to know God intimately as her Father. In her narrative she exclaims, 'Why can I say, *Father*? – Can I now at this time, with the confidence of a child, and without the least misgiving of heart, call God my Father?' This propelled her into a season of solitude in which she sought more of the 'silent and soft communion' of *Abba* Father. In the end it was the comfort of Romans 8.35 – 'Who shall separate us from the love of Christ?' – which led to her breakthrough: 'Melted and overcome by the sweetness of this assurance, I fell into a great flow of tears, and could not forbear weeping aloud. It appeared certain to me that God was my Father, and Christ my Lord and Savior, that he was mine and I his. Under a delightful sense of the immediate presence and love of God, these words seemed to come over and over in my mind, "My God, my all; my God, my all." The presence of God was so near, and so real, that I seemed scarcely conscious of anything else. God the Father, and the Lord Jesus Christ, seemed as distinct persons, both manifesting their inconceivable loveliness, and mildness, and gentleness, and their great immutable love to me.'

Sarah Edwards from this time on was blessed with these 'very intense religious affections' and had a profound sense of the transcendent love of God and 'his nearness to me, my dearness to him'. Put in the language of this book, she clearly experienced the Spirit of adoption and moved from feeling like an orphan (separated from the love of God) to a son/daughter (no longer separated, never to be separated again). For the full first-person account see <http://digital.library.upenn.edu/women/pierrepont/conversion/conversion.html>.

5 The orphaned angel

1 All quotations from Wesley's famous sermon on Romans 8.15, 'The Spirit of Bondage and of Adoption', are taken from the version edited by Brent Peterson, Ryan Danker and George Lyons, for the Wesley Center of Applied Theology (1999). This can be found at <http://wesley.nnu.edu/john-wesley/the-sermons-of-john-wesley-1872-edition/sermon-9-the-spirit-of-bondage-and-of-adoption/>.

2 Saint Augustine, *Questions on the Heptateuch* 2.73 (PL 34:623).

7 God's daughters and sons

1 For the most recent exploration of the nuptial metaphor, see Brant Petrie, *Jesus the Bridegroom: The greatest love story ever told* (New York: Image, 2014). Note that Martin Luther preferred to use the nuptial over the filial metaphor (in direct contrast to John Calvin). Luther wrote that 'faith unites the soul with Christ, as bride with her bridegroom' (Luther's Works, *Weimarer Ausgabe* 1.20.25). Luther's preference for the marriage metaphor over and against the adoption metaphor was rooted in his poor experience of being fathered.

2 Kharalambos Anstall, 'Juridical Justification Theology and a Statement of the Orthodox Teaching', in *Stricken by God? Nonviolent identification and the victory of Christ*, ed. Brad Jersak and Michael Hardin (Grand Rapids, MI: Eerdmans, 2007), 482–503, 488.

3 Anstall, 'Juridical Justification Theology', 488.

4 Anstall, 'Juridical Justification Theology', 488–9.

5 Anstall, 'Juridical Justification Theology', 492.

6 Anstall, 'Juridical Justification Theology', 499.

8 Why have you abandoned me?

1 Brennan Manning, *The Ragamuffin Gospel* (Colorado Springs, CO: Multnomah, 2005). Manning was one of the most poetic, mystical

and eloquent of the Catholic writers committed to the gospel of the Father's love, which is at the very heart of 'grace'. As a result of being baptized by *Abba*'s love, he wrote, 'I have been seized by the power of a great affection' (*Ragamuffin Gospel*, p. 35). Manning's own life, broken and flawed, gave him a very deep understanding of the Father's unconditional love, acceptance and compassion for human beings who feel like hypocrites because they never measure up to the legalistic requirements of religion. Manning famously said that 'the central revelation of Jesus Christ in the New Testament is that God is Abba, Daddy.'

2 This is a common critique, for example, of Peter Abelard's view of the atonement. Abelard's writings on the cross (found scattered throughout his commentary on Romans) are in part a critique of Anselm's satisfaction theory, which he disliked because it was based on a faulty understanding of God's justice (as retributive rather than restorative) and an inadequate attention to the love of God. For Abelard, the primary motivation behind the cross is rooted in what he called 'the perfection of love'. Love is the primary attribute of God, not 'justice' or 'righteousness'. Christ's love on the cross is accordingly the ultimate demonstration of God's perfect love, causing perfect love for God and neighbour to be 'enkindled' in our hearts. This then leads to freedom from fear (the prevailing human problem – living out of fear, as opposed to living out of love). This results in us enjoying 'the true liberty of the sons of God'.

Does this mean that Abelard saw Christ's death only as an inspiring example? On the one hand he does talk about Christ 'teaching us by word and example even to the point of death'. This led some rather carelessly to charge Abelard with 'exemplarism' (saying that the cross is merely an example, designed to inspire us to love). On the other hand, Abelard speaks of the cross achieving some kind of objective transaction and therefore functioning as more than merely an example. In fact, Abelard actually taught a version of what we would now call penal substitution. He wrote, 'There are two ways in which Christ is said to have died *on account of our sins*. First, the transgressions on account of which he died were ours, and we committed the sin whose punishment he bore. And second, by dying he took away our sins: that is, he removed the punishment for our sins at the cost of his death.'

9 A glorious homecoming

1 John Owen, *Communion with God, Father, Son and Holy Ghost*, ch. 4, at <http://www.ccel.org/ccel/owen/communion.toc.html>.
2 Owen, *Communion*, ch. 4.
3 Owen, *Communion*, ch. 4.
4 Owen, *Communion*, ch. 4.
5 Owen, *Communion*, ch. 4.

10 The heart of the gospel

1 Mark Stibbe, *From Orphans to Heirs: Celebrating our spiritual adoption* (Oxford: Bible Reading Fellowship, 1999).
2 For the few books written on spiritual adoption prior to mine, see Robert Alexander Webb, *The Reformed Doctrine of Adoption* (Grand Rapids, MI: Eerdmans, 1947), Brendan Byrne, *Sons of God, Seed of Abraham* (Rome: Gregorian University Press, 1979) and Sinclair Ferguson, *Children of the Living God: Delighting in the Father's love* (Edinburgh: Banner of Truth, 1989). A growing number of books have appeared since *From Orphans to Heirs*. In addition to those by Trevor Burke, please note Robert Peterson, *Adopted by God* (Phillipsburg, NJ: P&R Publishing, 2001) and R. W. Miller, *From Fear to Freedom* (Colorado Springs, CO: Multnomah, 2001), as well as Michael Milton, *What Is the Doctrine of Adoption?* (Phillipsburg, NJ: P&R Publishing, 2012). Saul Mateyu, *The Doctrine of Adoption* (Saarbrücken: Lambert Academic, 2012) should be mentioned too. For academic research into sonship and adoption, especially within the Roman world, see Michael Peppard, *The Son of God in the Roman World* (Oxford: Oxford University Press, 2012), H. Lindsay, *Adoption in the Roman World* (Cambridge: Cambridge University Press, 2009) and especially James Scott's exegetical study, *Adopted as Sons of God* (Tübingen: Mohr, 1992). Some seventeenth-century writers looked at spiritual adoption. See for example Thomas Granger, *A Looking-Glasse for Christians; or, The Comfortable Doctrine of Adoption* (1620). For the Puritan input on this subject see Joel Beeke, *Heirs with Christ: The Puritans on adoption* (Grand Rapids, MI: Reformation Heritage, 2008). For Calvin's contribution to the theology of adoption see Julie Canlis's excellent book, *Calvin's Ladder* (Grand Rapids, MI: Eerdmans, 2010).

3 John Wesley never wrote any works of systematic theology, but his sermons often touched on assurance of salvation. This caused Wesley to come back time and again to texts like Romans 8.15. See any collection of Wesley's sermons, trawl through them and enjoy his teaching on the Spirit of adoption – teaching that is not dry and academic but most often experiential and heartfelt.

4 J. McLeod Campbell, *The Nature of the Atonement* (Edinburgh: Handsel Press, 1996). The original edition, without an Introduction, was published in 1856 (Cambridge: Macmillan).

5 Campbell, *Nature of the Atonement*, ch. 15, 238.

6 Campbell, *Nature of the Atonement*, ch. 15, 239.

7 Campbell, *Nature of the Atonement*, ch. 15, 241. The italics are Campbell's.

8 Campbell, *Nature of the Atonement*, ch. 15, 243.

9 Campbell, *Nature of the Atonement*, ch. 15, 243. The italics are Campbell's.

10 Campbell, *Nature of the Atonement*, ch. 15, 245.

11 Campbell, *Nature of the Atonement*, ch. 8, 164.

12 Campbell, *Nature of the Atonement*, ch. 8, 166.

13 Campbell, *Nature of the Atonement*, ch. 8, 165.

14 Jonathan Sacks, 'Two Concepts of Teshuvah' (2007), <http://www.rabbisacks.org/nitzavim-5767-two-concepts-of-teshuvah/>.

15 See Norman Kraus, *Jesus Christ Our Lord: Christology from a disciple's perspective* (Eugene, OR: Wipf & Stock, 2004), first published in 1988. See also Mark Baker and Joel Green, *Recovering the Scandal of the Cross: Atonement in New Testament and contemporary contexts* (Downers Grove, IL: IVP Academic, 2000), ch. 6.